Nathalie Babel Brown received her Ph.D. from Columbia University. Her previous books include Isaac Babel, *The Lonely Years 1925-1939* and Isaac Babel, *You Must Know Everything*. She currently teaches Russian literature at the University of Ottawa.

Nathalie Babel Brown

HUGO &

DOSTOEVSKY

Introduction by Robert Belknap

ardis / ann arbor

Nathalie Babel Brown

Hugo and Dostoevsky

Copyright © 1978 by Ardis.
ISBN 0-88233-268-6 (cloth)

Published by Ardis,
2901 Heatherway,
Ann Arbor, Michigan 48104

Cover and jacket designed by
Gretchen Schneider.

For my aunt, Meri Babel Chapochnikoff,
For my uncle, Dr. Grégoire Chapochnikoff.
With so much love.

CONTENTS

INTRODUCTION

For more than a century, readers have examined, praised, and attacked Dostoevsky as a religious, political, or psychological commentator on his times, as an eccentric whose own nature and experiences fill and form his works, and as the prophet of the Russian, Freudian or Existentialist revolutions. Each of these critical traditions contains a strain of truth and a strain of fuzziness. A tougher-minded and more exciting tradition dates back to a challenge Leonid Grossman issued to the scholarly world over sixty years ago. Grossman presented Dostoevsky as a shrewdly self-conscious practitioner of the art of novel-writing, a man who set out to learn the genre from the finest writers of his time, and who deserved to be studied as a member of a literary community.

This study has proved exciting because an extraordinarily diverse and brilliant community of authors was inventing and exploiting a new kind of novel in nineteenth-century Europe. On foundations established by Cervantes in Spain, Goethe in Germany, Rousseau in France, and Sterne and his predecessors in England, this new school offered Dostoevsky an achievement comparable in its impact to that of Athenian drama or Renaissance painting. And Dostoevsky took pride in the sweep of sources in this community that he used. He boasted of reading of E.T.A. Hoffmann in Germany, translated Balzac from the French, adapted scenes and characters from Dickens's England, and was both praised and blamed in his own time for writing so much in the style of his compatriot, Gogol.

This vision of Dostoevsky as a literary craftsman, learning, adapting, and developing an established collection of novelistic techniques and materials, has shocked those who believe that novels emerge from the recesses of our tortured souls in much the same way as babies are flown in by storks. Literature, however, has always been a social enterprise, and the best writers have always made their inheritance their own by processes of imitation, parody, and misprision which critics are only beginning to understand. The center of the creative process remains mysterious, but this book shows how richly intricate it is. The old-fashioned search for sources no longer ends with their discovery; one source leads a scholar to another, for an author can compound materials from many sources in such a way as to turn another author's dross into gold. The psychology of creation used to be as mysterious as alchemy, but gradually scholars are finding laws like those of chemistry to describe it. And chemists really can come closer to the vital heart of nature. Dr. Babel Brown's book presents Dostoevsky's own sense that *Les Misérables* was a better novel than *Crime and Punishment*. Since modesty was not one of his conspicuous vices, Dostoevsky's humble admiration was probably sincere. It was certainly not blind; he pointed out the flawed love story in Hugo's work, but did not let that flaw reduce his appreciation of the whole. Babel Brown's book presents the real proof of Dostoevsky's sincerity—the multiplicity of points at which *Crime and Punishment* imitates *Les Misérables*. Dostoevsky expressed his admiration for Hugo before and after writing his own novel, but he embodied that admiration in the structure of his plot and the nature of his characters. Indeed Babel Brown finds the most important departure from Hugo's cast of central characters in the very role that Dostoevsky had deprecated in *Les Misérables*, the lover. After reading Dostoevsky's correspondence, one could suggest a source far removed from Hugo for the energetically lovesick Razumikhin: Fyodor Dostoevsky himself. His letters to his brother Mikhail about their joint publishing ventures contain far more of Razumikhin's racy literary practicality than they do of Raskolnikov's exacerbated introspection.

After showing how Dostoevsky read, judged, and adapted Hugo's plot and characters, Babel Brown examines the most eerily moving, most "Dostoevskian," most "Russian" passages in *Crime and Punishment,* Raskolnikov's two elaborately narrated dreams. She shows how the analogous scenes function in *Les Misérables* and why Dostoevsky altered them and merged them as he incorporated them into his text. Other works by Hugo and other authors enter the complex here, but the discourse comes to focus on the differences in nature between the two novels. Hugo was writing an examination of the implications of punishment, much as Dostoevsky had done in *The House of the Dead.* In *Crime and Punishment,* however, as Babel Brown shows, Dostoevsky carries the process one step further back and examines the ways in which punishment itself is implicit in crime. The study of the relationship between the two novels illuminates the nature and the goals of both.

The study of literature knows only arbitrary boundaries. All scholars and critics select the hundreds of literatures they will ignore or absorb at second hand because they lack the languages. Most also select an approach, and concentrate on the history of forms or ideas, the psychology of creation, the structure of a text, or any of the other approaches that are current at a given time. The best critics set boundaries upon their fields regretfully, in deference to human finitude; their epigones rejoice in limitations.

This book moves among these areas of literary study, applying their methods as the body of materials demands. It goes back to the hard facts that underlie our theories and histories of literature; it clarifies our understanding of two great masters, and it illuminates the development of one of mankind's major achievements, the novel in nineteenth-century Europe.

Robert Belknap

HUGO & DOSTOEVSKY

PREFACE

Hugo and Dostoevsky have been viewed as moral predecessors of the modern age. Yet until now no systematic study has been made of the link between these two authors. Such an investigation recommends itself on several counts. First, as major figures of nineteenth century fiction, a detailed comparative analysis of the two has an intrinsic literary critical interest. Further, as one writer was essentially a social critic and the other essentially a metaphysical moralist, their works represent a privileged situs for revealing the two archetypical modes of prophetic consciousness. Finally, there are many echoes of Victor Hugo's works in various novels of Dostoevsky, and the Russian himself acknowledged his indebtedness to his French contemporary. Yet, while borrowing material, Dostoevsky transforms it to serve his own structural and thematic needs. These borrowings and transformations afford an unusual opportunity for analysis of the techniques of fiction, an analysis that is also a commentary on the question of intrinsic versus contextual meaning in the theory of literary creation.

This study focuses on that novel by Dostoevsky, *Crime and Punishment*, which is richest in parallels with Victor Hugo's *Les Misérables*. Literary materials borrowed from Hugo are examined in terms of their transformation and absorption into the Dostoevskian context. Structural similarities between the two novels also are analyzed, with specific reference to the main plots, subplots, characterizations of the heroes, external and internal actions, time spans, and the Svidrigaylov/Raskolnikov, Thénardier/Jean Valjean relationships. It is then shown how the particular form of prophetic conscience of each of the authors is articulated in and determined through the form of his novel.

In addition to the visionary nature of the novels as a whole, each author makes use of dreams as prophetic devices *within* his novel. In order to reveal the difference between their modes of awareness, an examination is made of Raskolnikov's first dream, on the death of the horse. A remark by Ivan in *The Brothers Karamazov* suggests that Nekrasov's poem "About the Weather" served as the inspiration for this dream sequence. But Nekrasov's poem itself turns out to be partially a translation from Hugo's "Melancholia." Dostoevsky's portrayal of the dream scene thus represents a skillful composite of Hugo's and Nekrasov's poems. Likewise, an analysis of Raskolnikov's third dream, on the murder of the old pawnbroker, reveals that it is a compound of two dream scenes from Hugo's works, one from *Le Dernier Jour d'un Condamné*, the other from *Les Misérables.* Through these analyses it is shown how such material, though borrowed, is made to assume new intrinsic meaning within the context, psychology, and characterizations of the Dostoevskian novel. For all their apparent dissimilarities, *Crime and Punishment* and *Les Misérables* represent variations on a single structure and are drawn from the same fund of symbolic resources. The major differences between these two novels, as with other works by these authors, are determined by the difference in each author's ideology and purpose: Hugo was writing a novel that foreshadowed a century of social protest; Dostoevsky's psychological novel prefigures the alienation of modern man.

* * *

The initial idea for this project germinated years ago in a seminar held by Robert Belknap at Columbia University. Dr. Belknap had encouraged foreign students to look for possible relationships between Dostoevsky and great writers of their respective countries. As far as French literature was concerned, Balzac, Gide, Sartre and Camus came immediately to mind. Connections with Hugo were less obvious and, although the French author's name kept appearing in Dostoevsky's correspondence, little research had been done to explore this relation. The challenge unfolded and I decided to make this my dissertation topic.

Throughout my work on this project Robert Belknap has been my guide, mentor, and friend. From inception to completion he gave unstintingly of his knowledge, time and personal support. He has been an inspiration and a model for humane scholarship and the life of the mind. For all this I am greatly in his debt.

Whatever merit my writing on Hugo may have, credit is due to Michael Riffaterre, who accepted the joint sponsorship of my thesis. Professor Riffaterre's extraordinary erudition and his remarkable cognizance of Russian letters were invaluable, as were his critical comments and insistence on analytic rigor. With two such teachers it is hardly necessary to point out that failings in this text can only be mine.

Professors Carolyn Heilbrun, Helen Reguiero, and Robert Maguire completed my doctoral committee, and each of them encouraged me with their interest, suggestions, and openmindedness. It was my good fortune that Max Hayward was in New York while I was preparing original translations of the Russian texts and quotations.

I am extremely grateful for his help in rendering these materials into English.

During the period when I was still formulating my basic argument, I taught a seminar at the University of Texas in Austin. Skeptical students became detectives in their own right and began tracking down suspicious parallels between *Crime and Punishment* and *Les Misérables*. The work of Lorelei L. Norvell, Lois Field, and Scott Andrew Buchan was especially imaginative and useful.

Jacques Catteau, Donald Fanger, Stanford Lyman, and Louis Marin read the complete draft and made suggestions for improving it that I was happy to follow. My husband, Richard H. Brown, helped in more ways than I could mention here. However, I wish to thank him for his valuable editorial assistance and for having typed various drafts of the manuscript. Finally, I would like to extend my appreciation to Carl Proffer for bringing to the public a monograph of a controversial nature at a time when such an undertaking finds more nay-sayers than champions.

Nathalie Babel Brown
Washington, D.C., 1977

4

HUGO & DOSTOEVSKY

IN SEARCH OF A FORGOTTEN RELATION

> "A starving young man with an axe under his jacket.
> Who knows what Dostoevsky went through while he was in-
> venting this Raskolnikov of his. The name alone! I believe,"
> Bunin went on, dropping his voice, "that in those moments
> Dostoevsky was himself Raskolnikov. I hate your Dostoev-
> sky," he suddenly exclaimed again, passionately. "An utterly
> revolting writer with all his heaping of one thing on top of
> another, the ghastly carelessness of his completely affected,
> unnatural language that no one ever spoke or speaks, with all
> those importunate, wearisome repetitions, prolixities and
> sheer inarticulacy. . . . He keeps grabbing you by the ears and
> pushing your nose into this impossible mess he has invented,
> into a kind of mental vomit. And besides, it's so mannered,
> so artificial, so unnatural. The legend of the Grand Inquisi-
> tor!" Bunin cried with a grimace of disgust, and burst out
> laughing.

> *Valentin Kataev,* The Grass of Oblivion

> C'est lui, la cime encore à demi cachée, le noeud mystérieux
> de la chaîne; quelques-uns des plus généreux fleuves y pren-
> nent source, où les nouvelles soifs de l'Europe se peuvent ab-
> reuver aujourd'hui.

> *André Gide,* Dostoievsky

"Voici venir le Scythe, le vrai Scythe, qui va révo-
lutionner toutes nos habitudes intellectuelles." When
with these words Melchior de Vogüé (1848-1910) introduced Dostoevsky to the French in 1886,[1] he prophe-
sied and set the tone for the response to the Russian
writer in the West. In his long essay devoted to "cette
étrange figure," de Vogüé warns of the impossibility of
appraising—according to ordinary cannons of thought—

7

a writer whose works were so foreign to contemporary values and tastes: "Il faut considérer Dostoïevsky comme un phénomène d'un autre monde, un monstre incomplet et puissant, unique par l'originalité et l'intensité"(p. 267).

This view of Dostoevsky as a phenomenon for whom any established method of analysis would be unsuited was still held by John Middleton Murry, who wrote in 1924: "Our old methods and standards are useless to elucidate and to measure Dostoevsky, not because he is greater than the heroes of art who went before him, but because he is profoundly different."[2] Dostoevsky's fictional characters, in turn, "pass beyond human comparison, and are no longer to be judged by human laws."

Dostoevsky has, of course, been discussed by more temperate voices, but it still may be said that, in approaching him and his art, often a diffuse notion persists that one is in the presence of a "monstre sacré" whose "uniqueness" has to be accepted as *sui generis*. It is in this light that John Cowper Powys writes as late as 1946:

What we must aim at doing, it seems to me, in this great problem of Dostoievsky's experience of life confronted by the demonic energy of his genius, is to sweep away at one stroke the particular influence of this or that person upon him, for all such influences were—aye, I am sure of it!—unimportant, negligible, next to nothing, and to concentrate upon his whole objective *mass of experience* at any given moment and to watch the spectacle of this "Samson Agonistes" wrestling with a cosmogonic antagonist that is part animate and part inanimate![3]

Such energetic declarations have not prevented less apocalyptic and more trustworthy examination of

8

Dostoevsky's life and work. Since World War I, few novelists have received as much attention in Western Europe and the United States as Dostoevsky.[4] But however varied and numerous the responses to Dostoevsky's novels, the originality of his creation has set him apart in the view of many critics from the sum of European literature. Critical and scholarly books on Dostoevsky's debt to Russian, German, French or English literature are scarce. The interest shown by Russian scholars of the 1920s and early 1930s in investigating the mechanism of national and foreign influences on Dostoevsky's writing[5] has found but few and recent echoes.[6] In 1928 the eminent Dostoevsky specialist A.S. Dolinin (1885-1969) remarked that: "The question of the relationship between Dostoevsky's work and that of Hugo has, for all practical purposes, not yet even been treated systematically."[7] Though some fragmentary progress has been made in the last forty years, Dolinin's assertion is still valid, in that the line of research he suggested remains largely unexplored.

The present work is an attempt to remedy this situation by examining a literary relationship between Dostoevsky and Hugo. To do this is not to doubt the genius of Dostoevsky; rather this approach might illuminate the complexity of his creative process and technique.

By way of introduction we will document specifically the exposure Dostoevsky may have had to Hugo, and trace the critical and bibliographic record on the subject. This will provide a basis for discussing some hitherto unexplored points in the following chapters.

* * *

Dostoevsky's correspondence provides documentation of his lifelong interest in Victor Hugo. At the age of seventeen, while still a student at the St. Petersburg Military Engineering Academy, Fyodor wrote to his brother Mikhail on August 9, 1838:

You are boasting about having read a lot . . . but I ask you not to imagine that I am jealous of you. As for me, I have read in Petersburg at least as much as you. All of Hoffman . . . almost all of Balzac . . . Goethe's *Faust* . . . also [all of] Victor Hugo except *Cromwell* and *Hernani*. (Vol. I, p. 47)[8]

This is the first time Dostoevsky mentions Hugo's name. A few months later in another letter to his brother, dated October 31, 1839, Dostoevsky takes Hugo's side against the French critic Désiré Nisard,[9] whose article had appeared in Russian translation in a leading conservative journal:

I read recently in *The Son of the Fatherland [Syn otechestva]* an article on Victor Hugo by the critic Nisard. Oh, how low he [Hugo] stands in the opinion of the French! How Nisard presents his dramas and novels as insignificant! How unfair they [the French] are toward him, and Nisard (although an intelligent man) just tells lies! (Vol. I, p. 59)

In these years the brothers' correspondence was filled with fiery discussions about literary matters. The following lines, dated January 1, 1840, are part of a digression on the world's greatest poets:

Victor Hugo, as a lyricist, has a clearly angelic character, a Christian childlike tendency in his poetry, and in this nobody compares with him, not Schiller (no matter how Christian a poet Schiller may be), not the lyricist Shakespeare (I read his sonnets

10

in French), not Byron, not Pushkin. Only Homer, with that same unshakeable confidence in his calling, with his innocent faith in the god of poetry whom he served, resembles Victor Hugo in his use of poetry's sources; only in this use though not in thoughts. (Vol I, p. 58)

Some twenty years elapse between the letter quoted above and the reappearance of Hugo's name in Dostoevsky's writing. What happened to the young Russian during these two decades is literary history.[10] Having graduated in August 1843 from the Engineering School, Dostoevsky entered Government service in the Petersburg Engineering Department of the Ministry of War. As Avrahm Yarmolinsky puts it: "The service was as distasteful to him as school had been. It was indeed, intolerable. He compared it to a diet of potatoes."[11] By September 1844, less than a year later, he had given in his resignation and "joined the goodly company of those who have become great writers under the driving lash of poverty."[12]

Although Dostoevsky did not achieve instant greatness, his first book brought him immediate recognition and success. The story of his book *Poor Folk [Bednye Lyudi]* (published in January 1846), his discovery by Grigorovich, Nekrasov and Belinsky, and his dramatic entrance upon the literary stage make this episode in Dostoevsky's life one of the most famous moments in the history of Russian letters. The subsequent three years of financial crises and feverish literary activity, the progressive and painful estrangement from the literary circles that hailed his talent so enthusiastically and now received his work with increasing coldness, the periods of creativity and well-being alternating with ones of nervous disorders and general wretchedness—all these

11

pale, in the perspective of time, when one knows what befell Dostoevsky in his twenty-eighth year. On April 23, 1849, Dostoevsky was arrested along with 34 other members of the Petrashevsky circle.[13] Eight months of solitary confinement in the Peter-and-Paul Fortress, the mock execution by shooting, four years of hard labor in Siberia and four more as a private in a Siberian battalion —all this had to be endured before Dostoevsky was given permission to return to St. Petersburg in December 1859, just ten years after he had left Petersburg a prisoner in iron chains.

"For ten years," writes E.H. Carr, "Dostoevsky was cut off from the literary world; and when he once more emerged, the spiritual environment of the Russian man of letters had been so profoundly changed, and the new impressions which he had himself amassed were so powerful and so engrossing, that he found himself in the position of a man beginning a new career rather than of a man resuming an old one."[14] It is noteworthy, in the light of our thesis, that Hugo's name reappears in Dostoevsky's writings soon after the beginning of this "new career," during which the promising young writer of the 1840s developed into one of the greatest novelists of the nineteenth century.

One of Dostoevsky's first literary undertakings upon his return to the capital was the founding of *Time [Vremya]*, a literary magazine for which his brother served as official owner and manager. The first issue came out in January 1861, and as A.L. Bem has noted in his article "Hugo and Dostoyevski: A Literary Survey":

As of 1861, we find in his work and in material on his life a whole series of evidence that Dostoyevski read Hugo. Hugo's

12

name is mentioned as early as the January issue of *Vremya*, in which Dostoyevski began his career as a critic. In the same issue, Dostoyevski, in a note to N.N. Strakhov's article "Remark on a Line in a Newspaper" ["Zametka na odnu gazetnuyu strochku"], defended Hugo, along with other Western writers, against Russian criticism, which in his opinion spoke of them "extremely condescendingly because they did not fit the standards of our much too realistic criticism of that time."(p. 74)[15]

During the summer of 1862 Dostoevsky was able for the first time to realize an old wish to journey abroad. He left Russia on June 7, 1862, and for some eight to ten weeks traveled to Berlin, Paris, and London and then to Italy via Switzerland.[16] In Geneva he met his friend Strakhov, and the two went to Florence for a week. There Dostoevsky comported himself in his usual unorthodox fashion. "Fyodor Mikhailovich," writes Strakhov in his "Reminiscences," "was no great master in the art of traveling. . . ."

. . . He was not particularly interested in nature, nor in historical monuments nor in works of art, with the exception of the greatest; all his attention was concentrated on people. . . . And indeed we did not visit anything but only walked, where the crowd was thickest, and talked. . . . In Florence we spent a week in a small pension. . . . And there again we did not do anything as tourists do. Aside from walking the streets we were busy reading. Victor Hugo's novel *Les Misérables* had then just been published[17] and Fyodor Mikhailovich was buying it volume after volume. After reading a book he would pass it on to me, and three or four volumes were, in such a fashion, read during that week.[18]

It appears that this intensive reading had an almost immediate effect. From September to December 1862, a Russian translation of *Notre-Dame de Paris* was published in *Vremya* in four monthly installments. To justify his editorial decision to republish Hugo's novel some thirty years after its initial appearance, Dostoevsky wrote a vibrant "Introduction from the Editorial Staff."

This piece of writing is not only an enthusiastic eulogy, but, more importantly, it illuminates the continuity between Dostoevsky's aesthetic and Hugo's ethical, "Christian," and artistic message. Although the "Introduction to *Notre-Dame de Paris*" is sometimes referred to in passing and briefly quoted,[19] it has not, to the best of our knowledge, been regarded as a link between the ideas of the Russian and the French writer nor as a basis for investigating Hugo's literary influence upon Dostoevsky. Since this is a key document, we take the liberty of quoting from the "Introduction" at length.

"Le laid, c'est le beau." [In French in Dostoevsky's text.] Here is the formula to which thirty years ago self-satisfied mediocrity thought to reduce the basic direction of Victor Hugo's talent, having falsely understood and falsely transmitted to the public what Victor Hugo wrote to explain his ideas.[20] It must be admitted, however, that Hugo was partially responsible for his enemies' mockeries, because he justified himself rather incoherently. And yet the attacks and mockeries long ago disappeared and the name of Victor Hugo has not died; recently, more than thirty years after the appearance of his novel *Notre-Dame de Paris, Les Misérables* appeared, a novel in which a great poet and citizen displayed so much talent, expressed such artistic completeness, that the whole world flew to his work, all read it, and the fascinating impression of the novel was total and universal. It had long been apparent that Victor Hugo's idea was not characterized by the foolish caricatures of a formula that we cited above. His idea is the basic idea for all art of the nineteenth century, and Victor Hugo, as an artist, was virtually the first prophet of this idea. This idea is Christian and highly moral; its formula is the rehabilitation of the fallen man, crushed unjustly by the yoke of circumstances, by the stagnation of centuries and by social prejudices. This idea

14

is the justification of those pariahs of society, humiliated and rejected by all. Of course, the [use of] allegory is inconceivable in such an artistic work, as for example, *Notre-Dame de Paris*. But to whom does it not occur that Quasimodo is the personification of an oppressed and despised French people of medieval times, deaf and disfigured, gifted only with a terrible physical strength, but in whom there finally awaken love and thirst for justice, and together with these, both consciousness of its own truth and yet untapped endless strength.

Victor Hugo is almost certainly the leading exponent of the idea of "rehabilitation" in the literature of our era. At least he is the first to have propagated this idea with such artistic force. Of course, this idea is not an invention of Victor Hugo alone; on the contrary, although it is fashionable to condemn our century, coming after the great models of the past, for not having contributed anything new to literature and art, this idea is, nevertheless, an inalienable accessory and perhaps an historical inevitability of the nineteenth century. This [judgment of our times] is extremely unfair. Follow all the European literatures of our era and you will see in all of them traces of this same idea and perhaps by the end of the era it will be embodied fully, totally, clearly, and mightily, in some such great work of art that will express the aspirations and characteristics of its time as completely and eternally as, for example, *The Divine Comedy* expressed its epoch of medieval Catholic beliefs and ideals.

Victor Hugo is unquestionably the most powerful talent appearing in France in the nineteenth century. His idea got underway; even the form of today's French novel can probably be attributed to him alone. Even all his enormous shortcomings are to be found again in the works of almost all subsequent French romantics. Now, before the universal and almost worldwide success of *Les Misérables*, it has occurred to us that the novel *Notre-Dame de Paris* has for some reason not yet been translated. It goes without saying that all of us have read him before in French; but we decided, first of all, that only those knowing French have read him; second, not all those knowing French have read him; third, they read him long ago; and fourth, and foremost, thirty years ago the number of people reading French was not very large compared to those who would have been happy to read him, but were unable to read French. But now the number of readers has increased to perhaps ten times that of thirty years ago. Finally, and primarily, this is all past history. Today's generation will scarcely reread the old stuff. We even think that this novel of Victor Hugo's is very little known to today's generation of readers. This is why we have decided to translate in our journal a mighty work of genius in order to acquaint our public with a most remarkable work of French literature of our time. We even think that thirty years is a span such that even for those who have read the novel once it would not be too burdensome to read it once more.

And so we hope that the public does not complain because we offer a work so well known to all . . . *by title.*[21]

It can hardly be emphasized more emphatically than Dostoevsky does himself that the reading of *Les Misérables* not only revived his youthful literary interest in Hugo, but also gave resonance to his more mature philosophic speculations. The themes of "the rehabilitation of the fallen man" and "the justification of those pariahs" who are "humiliated and rejected by all" could not leave him indifferent.[22] This may explain why the book held such immediate fascination. Indeed, it became a favorite of Dostoevsky's from then on, for after the initial reading in Florence he refers to it a number of times. For example, the following letter, dated January 1, 1863, St. Petersburg, was addressed to Dostoevsky's friend Alexander Petrovich Milyukov: [23]

Wouldn't you let me have, for Heaven's sake, *Les Misérables* for no more than one or two days? If not all of it, at least the beginning? If not the beginning the middle will do or any part. If not in French at least in any Russian translation. I need it for an idea, I am putting an article together. (Vol. I, p. 313)

We do not know what "article" might have motivated such an urgent request, but we do know that work
on *Crime and Punishment* started in July 1865[24] and
that the serialized publication of the novel appeared in
eight installments from January to December 1866 in
The Russian Messenger [Russky vestnik]. We also have
ample evidence that Dostoevsky's intense interest in *Les
Misérables* did not subside after the publication of his
own novel.

The year 1866 was a turning point in Dostoevsky's
life and career. "*Crime and Punishment* placed him beyond dispute among the greatest Russian writers and
stabilized his domestic life and, eventually, his financial
situation."[25] On Febrary 15, 1867, Dostoevsky married
the young woman to whom he had dictated the last two
parts of *Crime and Punishment* and on April 14 of the
same year, the couple left for a journey abroad that was
to last four years. In the *Diary* in which Anna Grigorevna meticulously recorded the daily events of their first
four months of traveling, she wrote, on June 1, 1867: "I
read *Les Misérables*, that wonderful work of Victor
Hugo. Fedya thinks extremely highly of this work and
is rereading it with pleasure. Fedya explains and eluci-
dates much about the nature of the characters of the
novel."[26]

It is again Dostoevsky's wife who informs us of his
rereading *Les Misérables* once more on March 21 and 22,
1874. In this case the reading was done under rather
unusual circumstances. For about two years after his return to St. Petersburg in the summer of 1871, Dostoevsky had been engaged in journalistic activities and edit-
ing Prince Meshchersky's weekly paper *The Citizen
[Grazhdanin]*. At the beginning of 1873 Dostoevsky
failed to comply with some minor censorship regulation

and was sentenced to two days in jail, which he found time to serve over a year later. Here is how Anna Grigorevna describes her husband's return home:

Fyodor Mikhailovich came back from jail in excellent spirits and saying that he had spent two perfect days. His cellmate—some artisan—slept for hours on end and my husband was able, without hindrance, to reread Victor Hugo's *Les Misérables*—a work of which he thought highly.

How good it is that I was locked up—he said cheerfully— otherwise I would never have had the time to recall the former wonderful impressions made on me by this masterpiece.[27]

This review of source materials leaves little doubt about the special emphasis Dostoevsky placed on *Les Misérables*. In this light, it is particularly interesting to learn that he did not hesitate to compare Hugo's novel with one of his own. In answer to one of his correspondents, a Mrs. Lurie,[28] Dostoevsky wrote, on April 17, 1887:

I myself like *Les Misérables* very much. It came out at the same time as my *Crime and Punishment* (that is, it appeared two years earlier).[29] The late Fyodor I. Tyutchev, our great poet, and many others, at the time considered *Crime and Punishment* undoubtedly superior to *Les Misérables*. But I disagreed sincerely and with all my heart, and I am still convinced now despite the general opinion of all the experts.[30] But my love for *Les Misérables* does not prevent me from seeing its most important shortcomings. Valjean is a delightful creation, and there are many characteristic and magnificent passages. I wrote about this in my *Diary [of a Writer]* only last year.[31] But on the other hand, how funny his [Hugo's] lovers are, how typical of the French bourgeois at their worst! How funny is the endless chatter and, in places, the rhetoric of the novel, but his republicans are especially funny—overblown and unrealistic characters. His rascals are infinitely better. Whenever he makes these fallen characters true to life there is always, on Victor Hugo's part, humanity, love and magnanimity and you did very well in noticing this and liking it; especially your liking of *l'Abbé Myriel.*[32] I liked that very much in you. (Vol III, p. 264)

It seems fitting that our examination of these primary sources be closed with Dostoevsky's response to an invitation to attend an International Congress of Literature, where he would have been certain to encounter French writers and critics:

Monsieur le Président[33]

Vous me faites grand honneur en m'invitant au congrès international dont nos confrères de Paris ont pris l'initiative.

Le but que vous proposez touche de trop près aux intérêts des lettres, pour que je ne me fasse pas une obligation de répondre à votre appel. Il y a en outre pour moi un attrait tout particulier dans cette *solennité* littéraire qui doit s'ouvrir sous la présidence de Victor Hugo, le grand poète dont le génie a exercé sur moi dès mon enfance une si puissante influence.

Je dois prévoir toutefois, que ma santé peut me créer des difficultés. Il m'est indispensable de faire une saison d'eaux, et je ne sais rien encore ni du lieu ni de l'époque que les médecins prescriront.

Je ferai tous mes efforts pour concilier cette nécéssité avec mon vif désir de prendre part au congrès. Mais ne disposant pas de mon entieré [sic] liberté d'action, je dois vous informer pour qu'en présence de cette incertitude vous décidiez s'il convient ou non de m'adresser une carte de delegué [sic].

Veuiller agréer, Monsieur le Président, l'expression de mes sentiments de haute considération.[34] (Vol. IV, p. 55).

* * *

19

The connection between these two men of letters has been explicitly stated by Dostoevsky, but it is left to literary scholarship to define and explain the precise nature of this relationship. To date, however, consideration of this question has been limited. The view of Dostoevsky as a writer particularly aware of the problems of form and demands of plot and structure[35] was held by the literary historian Leonid Grossman, and it led him to investigate Dostoevsky's literary "sympathies" and "antipathies" and to address the question of influences. Grossman's *Dostoevsky's Poetics [Poetika Dostoyevskogo]*, first published in 1925, focuses primarily on Dostoevsky's ties with the European novel. In the section entitled "Composition in the Dostoevskian Novel" ["Kompozitsiya v romane Dostoyevskogo"], Grossman indicates those he sees as Dostoevsky's "literary masters" —first, the English Gothic novel, the French *roman-feuilleton*, then later Hoffmann, Walter Scott, George Sand, Balzac, and Hugo. The question of Hugo's influence is stated in a brief but very convincing manner:

The ideological closeness between Hugo and Dostoevsky is apparent in many cases. The themes of "poor people" (Hugo has a poem "Les Pauvres Gens" written after Dostoevsky's novel[36]) of the "injured and the insulted," of protest against capital punishment, or the rehabilitation of criminals, and finally of preaching universal unity[37] —all these themes bring social motifs into the novels of Hugo and Dostoevsky and impart to them a wealth of material for psychological observation. But Dostoevsky paid no less attention to the complex architecture of Hugo's novels. He saw in it an author's eternal desire to arouse the reader's keen interest in his subject and to keep him in a state of extreme suspense. He noted all the means employed in the achievement of this main purpose: the laying on of colors more thickly, boundless exaggeration, the interplay of contrasts, the introduction of antithesis not only into the style but also into the ideas and images, the constant flow of extreme effects, the accumulation of extraordinary episodes and unexpected disasters, and lastly an enormous number of characters picked from the most diverse social groups—a diversity that gives the author wide scope to introduce the most extremely varied romantic adventures one after another with incredible speed.

The mixture of all kinds of narrative elements in *Les Misérables*—historical pages about Waterloo and the Revolution of 1830, the depiction of convicts, police spies, *grisettes*, bishops in the spirit of early Christianity, the impoverished visionary professing a cult of Napoleon (the general psychological portrait of Raskolnikov is strongly reminiscent of the hero of *Les Misérables*, Marius Pontmercy) and finally the variety of scenes of action—the galleys, the convent, a town with a million people, the Paris sewers, factories, battlefields—all this continued to make clear to Dostoevsky the need constantly to vary the scene, the action and personages of a novel which had philosophical purposes such as showing the paths from evil to good, from injustice to truth, etc.[38]

During the same year, 1928, Grossman, who unfortunately never returned to the question of a Hugo-Dostoevsky literary relationship, was taken to task by Alexander Tseytlin, who approached the question from the viewpoint of Marxist sociology. Tseytlin's article *"Crime and Punishment* and *Les Misérables*: Sociological Parallels" [*"Prestupleniye i nakazaniye* i *Les Misérables*: Sotsiologicheskiye parallely"][39] is to our knowledge the only work dealing exclusively and specifically with these two novels.

The author underlines that Hugo and Dostoevsky shared a "common social basis"—namely the bourgeoisie, whose "spirit penetrates the structure of both novels." Both writers, according to Tseytlin, were equally ignorant of the world of aristocracy, peasantry and working proletarian classes,[40] and both profoundly contemptuous of the middle classes. Their characters are *déclassés*, victims of social order such as poor civil servants and prostitutes and finally the "intellectuals" Marius Pontmercy and Raskolnikov, who both decide to "fight capitalistic society." There are, however, profound differences between the two works, and these differences stem from the fact that "the artistic methods of Hugo and Dostoevsky were antithetic." Hugo was a sociological writer, a champion of popular rights who called for social reform. His intent was in general at the expense of the individual. Dostoevsky, on the other hand, was an extreme individualist, foreign to the political arena of the day, and primarily concerned with moral and religious issues. All this is particularly apparent if one opposes the heroic behavior of Marius and his friends during the Paris insurrection of June 1832 to Raskolnikov's thinking. As Tseytlin notes:

Dostoevsky's heroes are devoid of this Revolutionary ecstasy. They sarcastically mock the slogan in which freedom, equality and fraternity are proclaimed under threat of death. They accept the *fouriériste* utopias neither with their minds nor with their emotions. The hammer of capitalism and the anvil of feudal survivals strike heavy blows at their social mode of being, crush and shatter their minds. Marius leaves his room in order to take part in a revolt that has flared up.[41] Raskolnikov remains inactive in his wretched hovel. Marius is aware of himself as a particle of the collective, Raskolnikov is a profound and convinced individualist. Dostoevsky is interested not in the social fate of the middle class but in the ethical self-awareness of its most educated representatives, not in the spectacle of political rebellion but in the revolt of the personality, not in the changing fortunes of the battle, but in the deep processes taking place in the psyche of underground man. Hugo is primarily a sociologist, Dostoevsky a psychologist. (p. 28)

22

This fundamental difference being stated, Tseytlin shows evidence of the interest of both writers in identical themes—crime and revolt, penal servitude, the plight of the big cities, prostitution—as well as in parallel dramatic situations—such as the criminal and the law, the criminal and his conscience. Indeed, this is done so convincingly that Tseytlin ultimately has some difficulty in defending his conclusion that a comparative study of *Les Misérables* and *Crime and Punishment* would be "doubtful," "irrelevant," and "dangerous."

If we took the traditional point of view we should speak of the influence of Hugo on Dostoevsky, otherwise we could not understand the similarity in the texture of the two. But here we are faced with a number of difficulties which basically undermine our hypothesis. How can we explain the presence in Dostoevsky of a number of extremely important discrepancies with Hugo, different treatment of similar themes and so forth? If the similarity is to be explained by "influence" then the difference should evidently be explained by "repulsion." But how could both things coexist in Dostoevsky? What were the reasons that made him reject certain things in Victor Hugo? Was this to be explained by a lack of "congeniality" in the two novelists? But various accounts by their contemporaries speak of the opposite. Evidently these reasons were implicit not in the personal relations between Dostoevsky and Hugo but in what conditioned these personal relations, in the approach of the two to the reality they depicted, in its objective content and in the psychological composition of their close apperception. This was precisely how things stood with Hugo and Dostoevsky. But once their social-psychological attitude to what they depicted conditioned these similarities and differences, it is senseless from the scholarly point of view to refer to the personal relations of the two writers, their sympathies or antipathies. That would simply confuse the question of influences, a question which is basically of a sociological nature.... Hugo and Dostoevsky were artists of the same social group. This explains the similarities in their novels. But this group found itself in differing social-historical conditions. This gives us the key to

23

establishing their dissimilarities. Talk about "repulsion" and "attraction" on this level is nothing more than precarious idealistic speculation. (p.51)

Ironically, apart from his socio-political theorizing, one finds in Tseytlin's article a valuable and often accurate basis to the hypothesis of structural and thematic similarities between *Les Misérables* and *Crime and Punishment*.

In 1929, V.V. Vinogradov published a collection of essays entitled *The Evolution of Russian Naturalism: Gogol and Dostoyevski [Evolyutsiya russkogo naturalisma: Gogol i Dostoyevski]* in which he notes that: "Victor Hugo's work was for Dostoevsky the artistic reality in which reigned aesthetic norms dear to him, and he often turned to it for material for his literary composition as one would to a friendly power.[42]

In the only section of his work dealing with Hugo and Dostoevsky, Vinogradov investigates such "material" —namely traces of Hugo's *Le Dernier Jour d'un condamné* in some of Dostoevsky's novels. Vinogradov considers his endeavor as only a small part of the research to be done. In his own ponderous style, he suggests a program of study:

> The connection between Dostoevsky's novels and the poetics of Victor Hugo—something authenticated by the Russian writer himself—is accepted by students of their work as a fact of individual creative psychology, or as an example of "correspondence" in the international history of the social-ideological novel. From neither of these angles has the question yet been historically explained or interpreted. Even the materials needed for a precise formulation of the question have not yet been gathered. The first task of the historian of Russian literature is to make clear the changeable forms in which V. Hugo is understood as a

24

peculiar artistic category of devices in the various schools and systems of the Russian literary linguistic milieu. The solution to this task may proceed in two basic directions: the gathering and historical interpretation of literary statements about V. Hugo's politics in Russian movements of various periods and the study of the semantics of symbols and the functions of devices associated with this or that literary system and with the name of V. Hugo. Against the historical background recreated by such means, the way in which Dostoevsky understood V. Hugo's work and his image as a writer will be revealed, and the principles of the relationship between the poetic systems of the two writers will be brought out in terms of the literary life of Dostoevsky's era. (p. 127)

Despite his forceful suggestions, no further effort has been made to validate or refute Vinogradov's plan for research. The Grossman-Tseytlin divergence in approach—stylistic versus ideological criticism—has found neither advocates nor arbiters, and "the connection between Dostoevsky's novels and the poetics of Victor Hugo" has been very much ignored. The last specific pre-World War II contribution to this question was written in 1935. A.L. Bem's article "Hugo and Dostoyevski: A Literary Survey," from which we quoted before, is as its title suggests, a summing up of the evidence of Dostoevsky's involvement with Hugo's work as well as a rapid listing of existing writings devoted to that topic. At the close of his survey, Bem expresses the hope that the "fiftieth anniversary of Hugo's death [in Paris on May 22, 1885] will give a new impetus to the study of Hugo's influence on Dostoevsky"(p. 86). Bem's expectations, like Vinogradov's before him, have not yet been fulfilled. In his "Index" to *Dostoevsky's Occasional Writings*, 1963, David Magarshak, translator and biographer of Dostoevsky, supplies the following information: "Hugo, Victor (1802-1885) French novelist and poet. His novel *Les*

25

Misérables was greatly thought of by Dostoevsky." Such a noncommittal remark does no longer reflect quite accurately the state of scholarship on the relationship between the two writers. In his recent *Dostoevsky: The Seeds of Revolt, 1821-1849*, Joseph Frank pays closer attention to the Russian's worship of Victor Hugo and suggests that it might have had significant consequences (pp. 108-110, 121). Fridlender's article (see fn. 22)—more an overview than a point of view—can be read as an encouragement to reopen the case to further investigation and analysis. Yet despite convincing evidence of a close literary relationship between Hugo and Dostoevsky, as well as much urging by critics that this relationship be closely examined, the works discussed above constitute the sum of critical scholarship that has focused on this problem to date.

The present work will explore the influences of Hugo's writing on that of Dostoevsky, specifically by examining parallels established by Dostoevsky himself between his *Crime and Punishment* and Hugo's *Les Misérables*. From virtually all aesthetic, and even popular, perspectives, both these works are bona fide "masterpieces of world literature" that, from the day they first were published, have never ceased to attract attention. "Paris, depuis six jours, lit et dévore *Les Misérables*," was the news written to Hugo by his close friend Paul Meurice on July 6, 1862.[43] "*Crime et châtiment* assura la popularité de l'écrivain. On ne parla que de cet événement littéraire durant l'année 1866; toute la Russie en fut malade," (p. 254) was the comment of Melchior de Vogüé, an observer not particularly partial to Dostoevsky. Critical interest in each case was followed by popular acclaim.

The responses and approaches to these two novels would fill more than one library shelf; the reader can choose amongst biographical, historical, sociological, ideological, political, philosophical, psychoanalytical, religious, and psychological interpretations. Yet none of this vast commentary examines in depth the relation of the two authors to each other since, as we know, comparative studies of Hugo and Dostoevksy have only been sketched or hinted at so far. In dealing with both novels simultaneously, the question therefore arises as to what method of approach should be adopted. An examination of the aesthetic principles implicit in each work, or the aesthetic impact they make on the reader, might yield—in terms of literary theory—an attribution of commonalities between the two authors. Or one could explore the social milieux of each writer and possibly explain—in terms of sociology of literature—Dostoevsky's enthusiasm for Hugo. A survey of the literary tradition to which each writer belonged might circumscribe —in terms of literary history—their resemblances and delimit a degree of "influence."

Les Misérables and Crime and Punishment both deal with poor people, prostitution, children as victims, the criminal and his punishment, crime as alienation, the ideas of expiation and redemption, and the battle between good and evil in man's soul. Yet, if taken out of the context of the literary works themselves, these parallel themes, problems, and issues in no way "belong" to either writer, or even to literary criticism as such. Rather, they must be recognized as parts of world social, intellectual and literary developments. To limit the comparative study of such vast themes and ideas to an examination of only these two authors would likely be both incomplete and inconclusive.

27

The literary critic needs all the help she can get from the historian, sociologist, linguist or aesthetician. But she should take as her essential concern the *uses* and *interpretations* of themes, principles, or traditions in specific works of literature, rather than the sources, nature, or history of such elements in themselves. The focus, in other words, should be on the literary work; the evidence of what that work says, and the means by which the author says it, are sought within the text itself.[44]

Literary criticism based on a close reading of the text is our aim. We therefore shall call upon external evidence only when needed to substantiate the internal evidence upon which our arguments will rest.[45] Dostoevsky's knowledge of and admiration for Hugo are the premises upon which our investigation is based. Our aim is not to prove that one novel is "superior" to the other. Our interest lies in showing the devices by which materials from *Les Misérables*, and from other works of Hugo, have been assimilated into *Crime and Punishment*, how they have been *absorbed* in such a way as to fit Dostoevsky's structural and dramatic purposes. *Les Misérables* will be considered only as a basic source to *Crime and Punishment*, which in turn will be examined from the viewpoint of how Dostoevsky made use of Hugo's material. The links between the two writers will be seen as the concrete compositional devices used to achieve specific effects within a specific frame. Hugo wrote a social novel of redemption attained. Dostoevsky wrote a metaphysical novel of redemption sought. How exactly was this transformation accomplished?

Systematization, nailing down the evidence, are scholarly requirements of such a project. But they have the built-in danger of reducing literature to some formal schema. To do literary criticism is to believe that literature is more than this. And literature itself presupposes a structure of belief that in part operates under the guise of a continual investigation of literary works. But, paradoxically, the more we learn about the specific phenomena of literary creation, the more we are convinced that the origins and ultimate meanings of literary works are essentially unknowable and "spiritual" in substance. Thus the present study, even while unmasking the naive spiritualization of Dostoevsky attempted by some romantic critics, in no way pretends to exhaust the mysteries of Dostoevsky's creative process. Yet from a close study of Dostoevsky's techniques and stylistic devices, there should emerge an insight into *why* Dostoevsky turned to Hugo—that is to say, an understanding not simply of a case of literary borrowing, but rather of an instance of human affinities which not only transcends Taine's postulate of *race, moment, milieu,* but also shows that imagination and talent respect few proprieties and acknowledge no frontiers.

AN ANALYSIS OF STRUCTURAL SIMILARITIES BETWEEN VICTOR HUGO'S LES MISERABLES AND DOSTOEVSKY'S CRIME AND PUNISHMENT[1]

> Structure, according to the Oxford Concise Dictionary, is the "manner in which a building or organism or other complete whole is constructed." It is not a matter of the building itself nor the materials of which it is composed. . . . It is a question of the way in which these materials are assembled and combined to obtain an object created for specific purposes and capable of satisfying well-defined functions.
>
> *André Martinet, "Structure and Language"*

> There is nothing relative about justice, as there is nothing relative about conscience. Indeed, justice *is* conscience but the conscience of the whole of humanity. Those who clearly recognize the voice of their own conscience usually recognize also the voice of justice. I consider that in all questions, social or historical (if we are aware of them, not from hearsay or books, but are touched by them spiritually), justice will always suggest a way to act (or judge) which will not conflict with our conscience.
>
> *Alexander Solzhenitsyn*, Letter from Ryazan, *1967*

In order to identify the basic structural similarities existing between *Crime and Punishment* and *Les Misérables* it will be useful to construct a model in which the relevant materials are organized into manageable components. The respective basic structures of each novel should then emerge, and similarities and differences should become visible enough to be isolated and studied. Readers of these two novels are confronted with a sizeable cast of characters, but some major figures have become so well known, even archetypal, that they come effortlessly to mind. The following list pairs such major characters on the basis of the primary roles they play and of their relationships with each other.[2]

> A: Jean Valjean—Rodion Raskolnikov: Central character of the novel; a criminal pursued by the law.

> B: Javert—Porfiry: The police inspector who makes it his personal goal to bring the criminal to justice and pursues him through the course of the novel.

> C: Cosette—Dunya: A young girl related to the central character.

> D: Marius—Razumikhin: Upstanding young man who meets and marries the young girl mentioned above.

> E: Thénardier—Svidrigailov: The unsavory character who injured the young girl, through whom he comes into contact with the hero of the novel. He learns the secret of the hero's crime and seeks to denounce him for his own selfish purposes, only to become, inadvertently, his benefactor at the end.

> F: Mme Thénardier—Mrs. Svidrigailov: Devoted to her husband with a love that admits no rationality, she is not hindered by him in her unjust treatment of the young girl.

> G: Bishop Bienvenu—Sonya: A religious person whose simple goodness leads the hero to repent his crimes.

Having reduced the characters to their fundamental traits, we shall now take a synoptic view of their dynamic functions within the framework of each novel respectively. The letters used below correspond to the names

31

in our previous list:

Crime and Punishment	Les Misérables
1. A becomes unfeeling towards other people, self-centered, and alienated from society.	1. A becomes unfeeling towards other people, self-centered and alienated from society.
2. A commits a crime against innocent people.	2. A commits a crime against innocent people.
3. A conceals his crime and tries to lead life as before, performing many acts of charity for the unfortunate.	3. The saintly G gives an example of great charity and self-sacrifice for A.
4. B, the police inspector, suspects that A is secretly a criminal and takes it upon himself to bring him to justice.	4. A repents, humbles himself, and is transformed into one who lives not for himself, but for others.
5. The young girl C enters the story, having recently escaped the insults and injuries of E and F.	5. A conceals his crime and tries to lead life as before, performing many acts of charity for the unfortunate.
6. E, F's husband, comes upon A, arouses A's disgust by his amoral spirit and poses a new threat to A and C.	6. B, the police inspector, suspects that A is secretly a criminal and takes it upon himself to bring him to justice.
7. An incident takes place which frees A from all persecution for his criminal acts, except for the dogged pursuit of B.	7. A confesses before the law to his crime, and a man wrongly accused is set free.
8. C meets and falls in love	8. An incident takes place

with a fine young man, D.

9. A, finding out about the love of C and D, helps them come together.

10. E finds out A's secret and investigates A's position to see how he could profit from his knowledge.

11. E gives his information about A to A's family under the pretense of trying to help, but is rejected in his attempt to gain remuneration for it.

12. E leaves the scene forever.

13. A confesses before the law to his crime, and a man wrongly accused is set free.

14. A's family, having learned both the good and the bad things he had never told them, forgives him and takes pride in him.

15. The saintly G gives an example of great charity and self-sacrifice for A.

16. A repents, humbles himself, and hopes to be trans-

which frees A from all persecution for his criminal acts, except for the dogged pursuit of B.

9. The young girl C enters the story, having recently escaped the insults and injury of E and F.

10. E, F's husband, comes upon A, arouses A's disgust by his amoral spirit, and poses a new threat to A and C.

11. C meets and falls in love with a fine young man, D.

12. A, finding out about the love of C and D, helps them come together.

13. E finds out A's secret and investigates A's position to see how he could profit from his knowledge.

14. E gives his information about A to A's family under the pretext of trying to help, but is rejected in his attempt to gain remuneration for it.

15. E leaves the scene forever.

16. A's family, having learned both the good and the bad things

formed into one who lives not for himself, but for others.	he had never told them, forgives him and takes pride in him.

These outlines admittedly are not very good. Neither one is complete, for some parts of each story were left out because they had no parallel in the other novel.[3] Both outlines are contrived and carefully worded, for the events they refer to often are different. Each outline notes minor aspects of one novel that are more important in the other. But despite these failings, the two outlines highlight the remarkable parallels that surface as the plots are broken into their basic units.

In view of these strong parallels, we believe that it is justifiable to discuss these two plots from now on as though they were made from the same basic material, arranged in somewhat different ways, shaped by each writer's stress in certain places and disinterest in others, with some (usually slight) additions or omissions.

* * *

In *Les Misérables*, three separate stories are included in the plot—a central conflict between Jean Valjean and Javert, and two subplots, the love story of Marius and Cosette and the harassment of Jean Valjean by Thénardier. This same division into three parts can be made in *Crime and Punishment*, although a number of changes may be observed. The main plot, the pursuit of the hero by the police inspector, is more in the foreground in *Crime and Punishment* than in *Les Misérables*. Although Javert's threat to Valjean always looms behind the story of his attempts to build a new life, it comes to the fore intermittently in short but brutal flashes. But in *Crime and Punishment* the story of the pursued criminal and the pursuing inspector is more constantly in the reader's mind.

The first subplot, the love story, stands in the foreground for a large part of *Les Misérables*, but its Russian counterpart, the love story of Rasumikhin and Dunya, receives much less attention. There is, however, a potential love story between the hero Raskolnikov and Sonya, the woman whose Christian love influences him to change his life. Dostoevsky's complete lack of eroticism in this love story transforms the emotions of these two characters into functional equivalents of the saintliness shown by Bishop Beinvenu toward Jean Valjean and the latter's response to it.

The second subplot is that of the outsider who finds out about the hero's crime. Svidrigailov here is a parallel to Thenardier. Like Porfiry, however, Svidrigailov keeps himself closer to the hero than had Thénardier. He is also more integrated into the story as a whole, since his knowledge of the crime is one of the factors which drives Raskolnikov to confess.

Thus the tripartite division that fits *Les Misérables* can also be applied to *Crime and Punishment*. The emphasis on the various parts is different but most of the structure and most of the characters correspond quite well.

The Authors' Purposes

For all the fundamental similarities between the two novels, we cannot overlook the evidence that Hugo's book is about the relationship between crime and punishment in society, while Dostoevsky's deals with the relationship of crime and punishment in an individual conscience. Yet this basic difference will appear in its proper proportion, and the remarkable extent of the similarities between the novels will be perceived, only in the light of the question: How closely, after all, could the books have resembled one another?

Hugo's brief introduction to his novel states explicitly the idea around which it was built:

> Tant qu'il existera, par le fait des lois et des moeurs, une damnation sociale créant artificiellement, en pleine civilisation, des enfers, et compliquant d'une fatalité humaine la destinée qui est divine; tant que les trois problèmes du siècle, la dégradation de l'homme par le prolétariat, la déchéance de la femme par la faim, l'atrophie de l'enfant par la nuit, ne seront pas résolus; tant que, dans certaines régions, l'asphyxie sociale sera possible; en d'autres termes, et à un point de vue plus étendu encore, tant qu'il y aura sur la terre ignorance et misère, des livres de la nature de celui-ci pourront ne pas être inutiles.[4]
>
> Hauteville-House, 1er Janvier 1862

In 1865, from Wiesbaden, where he had lost all his money gambling, Dostoevsky wrote an extraordinary letter to the publisher of the *Russian Messenger (Russki Vestnik)*, M.N. Katkov, to offer him the novel he was then working on.[5] Thanks to this famous document we have both a synopsis and a clear statement of intention of what was to become *Crime and Punishment*:

> It is a psychological account of a crime. The action takes place at the present time, in this year. A young man expelled from the university, a bourgeois by origin and living in extreme poverty, out of lightheartedness and instability of ideas, having surrendered to some strange "unfinished

36

ideas" which are in the air, decides to get out of his deplorable situation with one stroke. He decides to kill an old woman, a titular counselor's widow, who lends money on interest. The old woman is stupid, deaf, sick, greedy, charges exorbitant interest, is evil and oppresses another life, tormenting her younger sister who is working for her. "She is not good for anything," "What is she living for?" "Is she useful to any one person?" etc. . . . The questions drive the young man out of his mind. He decides to kill her, to rob her, in order to make his mother, who is living in the provinces, happy, to rescue his sister, who is living as a governess at some rich people's estate, from the lecherous advances of the head of that family—advances which threaten to ruin her—to finish his studies, to go abroad and then be honest the rest of his life, firm and unyielding in the fulfillment of his "humanitarian duty toward mankind." Which of course "will make up for the crime," if one can call crime an act against an old, deaf, stupid, mean and sick woman who does not know herself what she is living for. . . . He spends almost a month after that until the final catastrophe. There are no suspicions against him nor can there be. Then the psychological process of the crime develops. Insoluble questions arise before the murderer, unsuspected and unexpected feelings torment his heart. (Vol. I, pp. 418, 419)

These texts show clearly that each of the authors set himself to his task with a different purpose and a different philosophy in mind. The motive each author pursued in writing his novel, the message he sought to illustrate by it, greatly affected what he said and how he said it. By examing the author's purpose in writing, and by evaluating its influence on the stuff of the novel, we may prepare ourselves to judge the extent to which the one novel resembles the other. In so doing, we will be

37

able to gauge how closely the novels could possibly have come to one another, and thus how close in fact they are.

* * *

Victor Hugo's novel is one of social criticism. In this, as in *Le Dernier Jour d'un condamné* (1829) and in *Claude Gueux* (1834), his focus is on the harshness and injustices of the law. He shows himself to be against the excessive severity of sentences passed on criminals, the cruelty of hard labor, and the assumption obviously behind the French penal system that the prisons exist to punish, and not to reform, the offender. The special passports issued to prisoners, the laws restricting them, and most of all the attitude of the average citizen towards them, made reform and entrance into normal society almost impossible for a man who was once convicted of a crime.[6] Thus, *Les Misérables* depicts the persecution of a decent and useful citizen for trivial legal offences in order to show how widely law was separated from justice.[7]

Dostoevsky's purpose as he set about writing his novel was to show the corruption of youth by modern ideas and the sickness of egoism in us as the sources of transgressions. He also wished to show that the seeds of our redemption lay in our compulsion to find a way back to our natural and healthy state of selfless love of others.

> The truth of God and the law of the earth take their own, and he ends by being *forced* to denounce himself. Forced, even if he is to perish in penal servitude, in order to join humanity again; the feeling of isolation and separation

from humanity which he felt immediately after committing the crime has exhausted him. The law of truth and human nature have taken their toll. . . . The criminal himself decides to accept suffering in order to redeem his act. (Vol. I, p. 419)

Let us now look at the way these differences in philosophy affected the telling of the two stories.

* * *

To reduce the central plot of the two novels to the simple formulation that they tell the story of a criminal pursued by a representative of the law is to cover up a multitude of differences between them both in structure and in style. But such differences in these two stories are, for the most part, only reflections of the much greater differences in their essences. Thus in this central plot the two authors express their widely different intents: Hugo to show the injustice of the law administered to its letter, without consideration of individual circumstances, and Dostoevsky to show that there is a force in men beyond their control that goads them into harmony with their fellow men, and so to right and self-less conduct. The two subplots have only a minor and supporting role in presenting the author's point of view; the central message is carried by the story of Jean Valjean's persecution by Javert and of Raskolnikov's contest with Porfiry.

The Heroes' Spiritual Rebirth

Inspired by a model of true religious feeling and

complete selflessness, Jean Valjean and Raskolnikov both are converted from egoism to a spirit of self-sacrifice and sympathy for others. The regeneration of Valjean under the influence of Bishop Bienvenu and the conversion of Raskolnikov before Sonya in Siberia each represents major developments in a long and tortuous novel.

While these two points in the stories obviously are parallel in action, their placing and use in the plot could hardly have been more different. In *Les Misérables* the story of the hero's transformation comes at the beginning of the novel when the reader has just become acquainted with him. After nineteen years in the galleys of Toulon, the convict Jean Valjean has been released. On his march to the city of Pontarlier, where he is to report, he has to show his "yellow passport" everywhere he stops. As a result he is refused lodgings and food. While he is preparing to spend the night on a stone bench en route in the town of Digne, an old woman points out a small house where he might receive succor. Valjean knocks and is indeed welcomed; he is invited to the dinner table, addressed as "monsieur," and given a bed by a man whom he believes to be a simple country priest. In the middle of the night, "the bed being too good," Valjean awakens and, after some moments of a "hideous meditation," takes the priest's silverware and flees. When brought back by the police Valjean learns that the old "priest" is the Bishop of Digne, who reports that he had "given" not only the silverware, but also a pair of silver candlesticks that Valjean had "forgotten." The police are dismissed and Valjean remains free.

Jean Valjean, mon frère, vous n'appartenez plus au mal, mais au bien. C'est votre âme que je vous achète: je

40

la retire aux pensées noires et à l'esprit de perdition, et je la donne à Dieu. (p. 113)

So saying, the Bishop sends Valjean on his way, "en proie a une foule de sensations nouvelles." Valjean continues walking through the countryside when toward evening a child—a street singer named Petit-Gervais— passes by. While playing with some coins, he drops one where Valjean is sitting absorbed in thought. Valjean steps on the coin and chases the child away. Then, when getting up to go, he sees the coin stolen "par habitude et par instinct." Valjean desperately and vainly looks for the child:

Enfin, à un endroit où trois sentiers se croisaient, il s'arrêta. La lune s'était levée. Il promena sa vue au loin et appela une dernière fois: "Petit-Gervais! Petit-Gervais!" Son cri s'éteignit dans la brume, sans même éveiller un écho. Il murmura encore: "Petit-Gervais!" mais d'une voix faible et presque inarticulée. Ce fut là son dernier effort; ses jarrets fléchirent brusquement sous lui comme si une puissance invisible l'accablait tout à coup du poids de sa mauvaise conscience; il tomba épuisé sur une grosse pierre, les poings dans ses cheveux et le visage dans ses genoux, et il cria; "Je suis un misérable!"

Alors son coeur creva et il se mit à pleurer. C'était la première fois qu'il pleurait depuis dix-neuf ans. (p. 118)

From then on Jean Valjean ceases to resist; he abandons his old self forever.

Combien d'heures pleura-t-il ainsi? que fit-il après avoir pleuré? où alla-t-il? on ne l'a jamais su. Il paraît seulement avéré que, dans cette même nuit, le voiturier qui faisait à cette époque le service de Grenoble et qui arrivait à Digne vers trois heures du matin, vit en traversant la rue de l'évêche un homme dans l'attitude de la prière, à genoux sur le pavé, dans l'ombre, devant la porte de Mgr. Bienvenu. (p. 121)

We should notice that one of the episodes of Valjean's conversion—namely the incident with Petit-Gervais—will trigger and justify the police's renewed interest in him. From then on, the novel will concern itself simultaneously with the life of a redeemed man as well as with his flight from the law.

Only a few hours elapse between the moment when Jean Valjean perceives fully his situation and the moment when he kneels in full repentance at the Bishop's door. For Raskolnikov the same process will take considerably longer. In the last chapter of *Crime and Punishment* Raskolnikov, who has already confessed his crime to Sonya, is preparing to abandon his nightmarish flight from himself and from the law. Yet what he believes is driving him is not personal conviction of his guilt but the realization that he is unable, because of "his own baseness and incompetence," to reap the fruits of his actions and to carry out the humanitarian plans he had made before the "useful" murder of the old pawnbroker. Since he has not succeeded he will accept the shame of his failure. Thus Raskolnikov, his thoughts in total disarray, walks once more around the city:

He suddenly remembered Sonya's words: "Go to the crossroads, bow down before the people, kiss the earth because you have offended it also, and say aloud to all the world, 'I am a murderer.' " His whole body started trembling as he recalled this. And he was so crushed by the inescapable misery and torment of this whole period, especially the last few hours, that he threw himself into the possibility of this all-encompassing, new and complete sensation. Suddenly it had come down on him as a

42

trance: a single spark had enflamed his soul and, in one moment, like a fire, had caught his whole being. Everything in him softened all at once and the tears gushed out. He fell to the ground where he stood. . . . He knelt down in the middle of the square, bowed down to the earth, and kissed the dirty ground with pleasure and happiness. He stood up and bowed down a second time.[8]

Although Raskolnikov did not bring himself to say aloud to the crowd that had gathered, "I am a murderer," he does get up and take himself directly to the police station. His last hesitations are overcome when he sees Sonya standing in the courtyard, looking at him "wildly, desperately." He then makes his statement, "It was I who killed. . . ."

But Raskolnikov's moment of complete repentance will come much later. It will be another year, including some seven months of penal servitude in Siberia, before his final transformation. This conversion scene is not even a regular part of the story; it is told in the "Epilogue":

He himself did not know how it happened, but suddenly it seemed as if someone had seized him and thrown him at her feet. He wept and clasped her knees. For a second she was terribly frightened and her face grew dead white. . . . But all at once, in that instant, she understood it all. In her eyes shone infinite happiness; she had understood . . . that he loved her . . . and that now at last that moment had come. . . . (p. 573)

This very different placement of incidents otherwise so similar suggests the different points the authors tried to make by it.[9] As Hugo was trying to show the injustice of law when it is blind to the individual case and has the purpose only of avenging the crime rather than reforming the criminal, he had to change Valjean into a good man, even into an extraordinary model of virtue, before the story of his persecution by mechanical legality gets under way. Only thus could the gap between society's law and true justice be effectively highlighted. If Jean Valjean had not been presented from the very first as the sympathetic victim of society, if he had not repented completely and shown by his actions his willingness to serve his fellow man, the reader would have been less prone to sympathize with him, no matter how trivial had been his crime nor how disproportionately harsh the punishment which he faced. Hugo's message would then have been weaker and less explicit.

On the other hand, Dostoevsky's point is that some power in normal men forces them out of the unnatural egoism that engenders crime and leads them back to selfless unity with society. Yet this point scarcely could have been made if Raskolnikov's conversion had taken place as early in the novel as that of Valjean. The passage of nineteen brutalizing years before Jean Valjean comes to a full understanding of his position and of his choice serves as background in *Les Misérables*; yet it is the gap between Raskolnikov's initial realization of his crime and the resurgence of his feelings for mankind— and with it his capacity to love—which is not the background, but the subject of Dostoevsky's novel. Thus the eroding effects of conscience—the reckless hints calling attention to himself in the investigation, the feverish confessions of his guilt and the desire to share the secret with others, the constant fears despite the total lack of incriminating evidence—all this had to be shown in Raskolnikov, in his old self that is, before a new self could emerge. Had Raskolnikov been forced into his crime by misfortune or lack of forethought one might suspect that he would be more vulnerable to the guilt and

44

remorse he begins to experience shortly after the murder. But Raskolnikov entered the crime willingly, fortified by logic and conviction and determined to prove that he could keep control over himself. This very sureness of purpose in the criminal underlines the even greater power and certainty of conscience. Moreover, it determines that the conversion of Raskolnikov must of necessity come, not only at the end of the story of his chase, but even in the epilogue, after his attempts to rise above his conscience have been completely undermined. By his confession to the police Raskolnikov had done no more than admit that he is not an exceptional man, above his fellows and their weaknesses; but by repressing the impulse that seized him in the public square, he refuses to affirm his bonds with humanity and to abandon his separateness. It is only through his conversion at Sonya's feet, in his rediscovered ability to shed tears, that Raskolnikov finally gives up the egoism that had led to his pride and, consequently, to his crime. It is in his conversion, not his confession, that he trades willful isolation for a new life.

Thus the placing of the same action in the two works—the change in the hero from concern only for himself to a willing devotedness to others, certainly a major turning point in each story—was dictated by each author's purpose in writing his novel.

External versus Internal Action

Another difference between the two novels is the stress Hugo places on actual physical movement, as against Dostoevsky's internalization of the action. Javert's pursuit of Valjean is quite literal. He sees the convict in darkened rooms and chases him through alleys at night. For Dostoevsky, the pursuit is conducted through words and hints, a knowing smile, a pointed question, or a threat by Porfiry. Raskolnikov runs in circles but does not run away, nor does Porfiry give chase. Yet even this basic change follows necessarily from the difference in the purpose and message of the two authors.

Javert and Porfiry both personify legal power. Both pursue wrongdoers with extraordinary persistence and both reach their goal insofar as they finally trap the criminal.[10] But despite these functional similarities, they are profoundly unlike in their personal characteristics and psychological makeups and, consequently, in their methods and underlying motivations. Here is now Hugo presents Javert to his readers:

> Les paysans asturiens sont convaincus que dans toute portée de louve il y a un chien, lequel est tué par la mère, sans quoi en grandissant il dévorerait les autres petits.

> Donnez une face humaine à ce chien fils d'une louve, et ce sera Javert. (p. 178)

> Cet homme était composé de deux sentiments très simples, et relativement très bons, mais qu'il faisait presque mauvais à force de les exagérer: le respect de l'autorité, la haine de la rébellion; et à ses yeux le vol, le meurtre, tous les crimes, n'étaient que des formes de la rébellion. Il enveloppait dans une sorte de foi aveugle et profonde tout ce qui a une fonction dans l'Etat, depuis le premier ministre jusqu'au garde champêtre. Il couvrait de mépris, d'aversion et de dégoût tout ce qui avait franchi une fois le seuil légal du mal. Il était absolu et n'admettait pas d'exception. (p. 179).

For such a man there can be no greater joy than to capture one whom he sees as a rebel against authority. One night he knows that he is finally about to catch Jean Valjean who, fleeing into a dead-end street, will find no way to escape.

> Puis il se mit à jouer. Il eut un moment ravissant et infernal; il laissa aller son homme devant lui, sachant qu'il le tenait, mais désirant reculer le plus possible le moment de l'arrêter, heureux de le sentir pris et de le voir libre, le couvant du regard avec cette volupté de l'araignée qui laisse voleter la mouche et du chat qui laisse courir la souris. La griffe et la serre ont une sensualité monstrueuse; c'est le mouvement obscur de la bête emprisonnée dans leur tenaille. Quel délice que cet étouffement! (p. 492)

Porfiry, on the other hand, says of himself, "Who am I? I am a man who has developed as far as he is capable, that is all. A man, perhaps, of feeling and sympathy, of some knowledge perhaps, but no longer capable of further development"(Vol. V, p. 480). No wonder then that such a man would have perfected his own technique which Porfiry describes as follows:

> Now, if I leave one gentleman quite alone, if I don't arrest him or disturb him in any way, but if he knows every hour and every minute, or at least suspects, that I know everything down to the last detail, that I am keeping an eye on him day and night, watching him with ceaseless vigilance, if he always is aware that he is under constant surveillance and is afraid, then he is absolutely certain to lose his head and, truly, he will come of his own accord. . . (Vol. V, p. 353).

The three occasions on which Jean Valjean is cornered by Javert but manages to escape have their counterpart in *Crime and Punishment* in the three conversations between Porfiry and Raskolnikov. Yet the suspense in the Russian novel is due not to external and adventuresome elements, but to the extreme intensity of these verbal duels. Furthermore, Porfiry's dialectic is not aimed only at arresting Raskolnikov. In the same manner that he has "guessed" everything, he also knows that Raskolnikov, in order to regain his own humanity and to stop torturing himself, needs to submit to the justice of men and to their punishment.

Such psychological experimentation or higher motives never enter Javert's mind. To fulfill his "duty," which is to send an escaped convict back to the galleys, he watches, observes, indefatigably investigates year after year, but never stops to ponder on the humanity or the inhumanity of his task.

This difference in the external versus the internal attitudes of the police inspectors is reflected in the differing impacts they have on the two protagonists. Jean Valjean was transformed into a good man at the same time as his flight from the law began. Humility and service to others are now part of his nature. He feels indebtedness to individuals; it is his conscience that makes him twice confess, not the pressure of the law. Indeed, he twice gives himself over to the police, once when another man is about to be punished in his place and once when he frees Javert and gives him his address, because he has, by then, accomplished what he had set out to do and feels that his presence is no longer indispensable to the welfare of others. Having done his duty by saving another man, he feels free to escape, since the solution to his internal conflicts is not to be found in "lawful" expiation. Thus, the only possible form for the chase is a very physical one, expressing in the most concrete terms the tenacious persecution of a good man.

48

Dostoevsky, however, could not depict such a chase and still be true to the purpose of his novel. He had to maintain his focus on the dissolution of Raskolnikov's resolve, aided by Porfiry's perspicacity and eloquence. Too much physical action would have distracted the reader from his observation of the change in the hero's mind. The pursuit had to be carefully limited to those taunts and pinpricks that speed Raskolnikov's inner deterioration, but are never sharp enough to suggest that this deterioration is anything but the product of a purely internal force, Raskolnikov's conscience.

Time in the Two Novels

Closely related to comparisons of internal and external action is the difference of time span in the two novels. The flight of Jean Valjean from Javert extends over a period of some twenty years, as well it must, given the nature of the pursuit. Hugo could have placed a mass of physical action into a shorter period, but this would have been less effective in terms of what Hugo sought to express. Valjean can only show his good intentions when he is not running. Only through the passage of time can he perform those altruistic deeds that retrospectively make his initial criminal acts seem so small. Javert's effort to destroy this beneficent existence then can become an example of the blind stubborness of the law.

In contrast, Dostoevsky's focus on the inner struggle of his hero could hardly have stretched beyond the few weeks he depicts without losing credibility or weakening the impact of the conflict.

49

The way each author characterized his hero also was influenced by each hero's function in carrying his author's message. Valjean is portrayed as having been forced into crime by social injustices. He is depicted as being exceptionally intelligent, yet his thought processes are seldom pictured. As a result of his spiritual transformation early in the book, Valjean's thoughts focus on deciding what would be best for others, and resolving himself to follow that course of action. Valjean's almost total relinquishing of self derives from the author's desire to create a completely virtuous man who stands out all the more sharply against the unjust treatment meted him. Jean Valjean is almost too good to be real. That he elicits sympathy, that he is kind and generous, goes without saying. Indeed, Valjean is so much a figure to Hugo's purpose, created to fulfill the role of a kind, generous, and injured man, that one is bound to be on his side.

Raskolnikov is more complex, but even his character can be understood as composed of two basic components: the inclination toward goodness and self-sacrifice[11] that was all of Jean Valjean, and the unnatural spirit of rationalism and egocentrism. The first attributes are presented as the natural core of human personality, the second are shown as an artificial overlay. By turning all his thoughts inward, Raskolnikov eventually lost all contact and feeling for others. Out of his self-absorption he imagined that some men were above others and that he was one of these chosen few. *Crime and Punishment* is the story of the gradual dissolution of this outer layer and the triumph of the natural spirit of

50

human bondedness. Whether Dostoevsky's philosophic assumptions are correct or not, he created a highly dramatic character to embody and evince them. Raskolnikov was not built to fit a part in a story; instead, the story was constructed to show the way Raskolnikov was built.

The First Subplot: A Love Story

The three circles of action in the two novels are not identical, but the greatest divergence is to be found between the love story of Marius and Cosette and that of Rasumikhin and Dunya. The actual events are not changed so much as their relative importance in the novel as a whole. Marius's troubled courtship of Cosette receives at least as much space in *Les Misérables* as does the central plot, whereas the shy unfolding of love between Razumikhin and Dunya seems added almost as an afterthought in *Crime and Punishment*.

The romance of Marius and Cosette serves a useful function in *Les Misérables*. It forces the main plot, the chase, into the background for a time, and it reminds the reader that the hero is not only "cet homme qui avait été presque méchant et qui était devenu presque saint"(p. 912), but also that he is a vulnerable human being. Valjean, at first bewildered and frightened as he sees Cosette flower from girlhood to womanly beauty, experiences all the tortures of jealousy when he discovers that she is in love. The romance thus sets the stage for Valjean's most selfless choice: to give his daughter to Marius and, on the day after the wedding, to confess to him his past and thus bring on his ultimate ordeal—separation from his beloved Cosette.

51

The love story also marks the passage of time and creates a sense of peaceful sweetness and youthful hope, against which the reappearance of Javert seems even more appalling. Jean Valjean's crime is made in this way to appear all the more distant and trivial, and the sympathies of the readers are aroused not only for him, but for the hardships his persecution forces on the young lovers as well.

As for the love story between Razumikhin and Dunya, a study of *The Notebooks for Crime and Punishment* (which, of course, were never intended for publication) shows that this sub-plot is less explicit and less exploited in the finished version than it had been originally intended. In these *Notebooks*, which contain outlines and sometimes extensive drafts of chapters, sketches of characters and an abundance of observations on narrative development and motivation, we find the following entry:

Notes for the Novel (Jan. 2, 1866)
Characteristics

1.

Razumikhin

Razumikhin is a very strong character and, as often happens with strong characters, he submits entirely to Avdotya Romanovna. (N.B. He also has the feature often encountered in people—who though most decent and generous are rough and rowdy, *bambocheurs* who have seen much that is sordid—that for example he somehow humbles himself before a woman, particularly if this woman is elegant, proud and beautiful.) At first Razumikhin became the slave of Dunya; (a nimble young man, as his mother called him) he humbled himself before her. The very thought that she might be his wife at first seemed to him monstrous,

52

and yet he was boundlessly in love with her from the first evening that he saw her. When she allowed the possibility that she might become his wife, he almost went out of his mind (scene). Though he loves her terribly, though by nature he is willful and bold to the point of absurdity, and despite the fact that he is her fiancé, he always trembled before her and was afraid of her, while she, though she loved him, was spoiled, conceited, and ambitious, also at times seemed to despise him. He didn't dare talk with her. And therefore from the very first he hated Sonya, because Dunya also hated her and had insulted her (went too far) and quarreled through this with him. But later (beginning with the second half of the novel), having understood who Sonya really was, he suddenly went over to her side, and had a terrible row with Dunya, broke with her, and went on a spree. But when he learned that Dunya had visited Sonya, and so forth (and when he himself could not stand his own despair), Dunya found him and saved him. She now began to respect him more for his character. In one word, Razumikhin's character.[12]

As we know, very few of these complexities have found their way into the novel. These characteristics are but one example of the wealth of material that could have been developed into sub-plots of great length and intricate psychology, such as Raskolnikov's love-hate relations with his mother or his tense relationship with his sister who, in turn, was linked emotionally to Sonya. The most flagrant change, of course, concerns Raskolnikov and Sonya, whose passionate love affair is entirely sublimated throughout *Crime and Punishment*.

All these complications of plot and character were subsequently either omitted or considerably simplified. The differences between the *Notebooks* and the novel should show that Dostoevsky's concern was to keep the reader's attention on Raskolnikov's actions and reflections and that strong secondary stories—which might serve to gain sympathy for the hero or distract from his flight from the law—were suppressed.

The Second Subplot: The Outsider as Villain

The second subplot develops as a corollary of the first, for it involves one of the main actors of the first subplot, the girl particularly dear to the hero—Jean Valjean's adopted daughter Cosette—and Raskolnikov's sister Dunya. Since the outsider has an evil interest in the girl, he is a villain in the eyes of the hero. The hero's relationship with the villain therefore is antagonistic and is sustained by the latter, who in each case has something to gain from his villainy. In neither novel does the hero pursue the villain for purposes of revenge, punishment or satisfaction. Thus, Thénardier maintains an association with Valjean by attempting to blackmail him for lucre, while Svidrigailov, who would like Raskolnikov to bring him closer to Dunya, practices psychological blackmail. In both cases the hold which the villain has on the hero will accelerate the story's denouement.

The Encounters between Jean Valjean and Thénardier

There are four encounters between Thénardier and Jean Valjean. The first meeting occurred when, in order to fulfill the request of Cosette's dead mother, Valjean went to Thénardier's inn at Montfermeil and took the child away. This brief meeting was unimportant to Valjean, and he did not recognize Thénardier later in Paris until the innkeeper revealed his true name and the circumstances of their first meeting. This first acquaintance with Thénardier thus was colored by the man's cruelty towards Cosette, whom Valjean came to love, but it involved no closer contact with the man himself, and did no more than give Valjean the occasion to know and to dislike Thénardier.

The next meeting between these two is in a tenement in Paris. Thénardier, having recognized Valjean as the "rich man" who took Cosette away, holds him captive in order to extort money from him. This meeting gives Valjean even surer reason to hate Thénardier; it is the only occasion Valjean has to learn about Thénardier's character and of the threat he represents as an evil man who has guessed Valjean is a fugitive from the law. Although the author has given the reader much additional information about Thénardier, Valjean knows little more about him, the way he thinks and who he is, than what he learns from this second encounter.

The third time their paths cross is when Valjean is carrying Marius away from the barricades through the sewers of Paris. Valjean tries to conceal his face from Thénardier, and the latter at first does not recognize him. This incident serves to give Thénardier some special information about Valjean that helps drive the story to its conclusion.

The last influence of Thénardier on Valjean's life is played out through an intermediary, Marius, to whom Thénardier tries to denounce Valjean with the information he gained from their fleeting, third encounter in the sewers. Thénardier's plan to discredit Valjean fails unexpectedly and, indeed, the end result of his attempt is only to bring Valjean's story to a happy closure. Thénardier's final role is that of an unwitting benefactor, whose desire to exploit Valjean's secrets not only brings about his own banishment to America, but also erases the last suspicions that had separated Marius, Cosette, and Jean Valjean. Evilness is not abolished by these means, but it is made to undermine its own goal and used to aid the righteous.

Parallels in the Relationship of Svidrigailov and Rodion Raskolnikov and that of Thénardier and Jean Valjean

There are strong parallels between the relationship and encounters of Svidrigailov with Raskolnikov and those between Thénardier and Jean Valjean. The two dyadic relationships vary in their details, but a careful study will show the same basic pattern in each. There were four important encounters between Valjean and Thénardier, each of them serving to move the story along to a new stage. There are slightly more encounters between Raskolnikov and Svidrigailov, but they proceed through the same four stages with fundamentally corresponding effects on the plot.

Svidrigailov first enters the life of Raskolnikov before the two have even met. Raskolnikov hears about Svirdrigailov in a letter from his mother. Raskolnikov thus comes to know Svidrigailov only by his bad reputation, as the man at whose hands his sister has endured humiliation and suffering. This is approximately the situation after the first encounter between Valjean and Thénardier, when the former takes Cosette away from Montfermeil. In both cases the first links between these characters are forged out of their separate relationships to a third person whom one has abused and the other loves.

Raskolnikov actually meets Svidrigailov when the latter comes to visit him in St. Petersburg with the offer to help his sister Dunya. According to Svidrigailov, all he wants is an interview with Dunya—a chance to convince her that he regrets the harm he has brought her, to dissuade her from marrying Luzhin for whatever security that might bring, and to offer her money so she need not marry out of penury. This is the longest meeting between them, and the one in which Svidrigailov reveals most about his character to Raskolnikov. Despite the many differences in circumstances, this meeting corresponds structurally and thematically to that between Valjean and Thénardier in the Paris tenement. In both stories this second meeting was a consequence of the first indirect ties between these characters and, by it, the heroes of both novels see that the villains, whom they had considered as part only of their past, are going to pose a threat to them in the future.

The next series of contacts between Svidrigailov and Raskolnikov parallels Thénardier's chance encounter with Valjean in the sewers and the investigations and deductions Thénardier made in preparation for his attempt to denounce him. Svidrigailov also learns some secret information about Raskolnikov when he eavesdrops on his confession to Sonya and, in a series of minor confrontations he learns how easily Raskolnikov can be wounded by this knowledge. Thus, the action of the third encounter is in two parts. Hugo's novel, which moves through a series of unexpected shocks to the reader, stresses the chance encounter in the sewers and leaves Thénardier's detective work unknown until the surprise of the fourth meeting lets us see its results. Dostoevsky stresses the growing anxiety being built up in his hero, and underplays the actual gaining of information by Svidrigailov, not even describing his listening to Raskolnikov and Sonya from the adjoining room. By

57

this tactic Dostoevsky underlines the series of hints and probing encounters by which Svidrigailov learns how he can take advantage of Raskolnikov's position. This third contact between the two pairs, consisting both in the chance acquisition by the villain of information detrimental to the hero and in his discovery of a way to exploit it, prepares the stage for their final involvement in one another's lives.

Svidrigailov informs Dunya of her brother's crime and, whether planned that way or not, this meeting with her dissolves into a last, unsuccessful attempt to seduce her. Thus, as in *Les Misérables*, the villain's final influence is played out, not directly, but through a third party. Also, as in *Les Misérables*, the villain's attempt to profit from his information about the hero's crime fails, and he is himself removed from the scene. Thénardier is exiled to America as a result of his failure; Svidrigailov, claiming that he is going to America, shoots himself. In the end, each villain brings benefits to those whom they had sought to injure. Thénardier's "gift" was in the very information he brought;[13] Svidrigailov's was both in the material help he gave to Raskolnikov's family and in the force he applied to bring Raskolnikov to the healing expiation of his crime in Siberia.

The relationships of Svidrigailov, Raskolnikov, and Dunya, as well as those of Thénardier, Valjean, and Cosette, are summarized below:

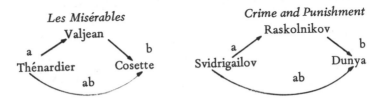

The above diagram can be read as follows:

a: Both Thénardier and Svidrigailov come to know the hero through their malevolent interest in the hero's loved one.

b: Both Valjean and Raskolnikov manifest their love for Cosette and Dunya by protecting them from Thénardier and Svidrigailov.

ab: Both Thénardier and Svidrigailov are involved with women of whom they wish to take advantage, but neither is successful. In the case of *Les Misérables*, Jean Valjean is in the way, and in the case of *Crime and Punishment*, Dunya is, ultimately, able to extricate herself from danger.

a, b, ab: The ousider as villain is thus transposed into a catalyst of both plot and denouement by his relationships with hero and victim.

The Paradox of the Outsider

Thénardier is immoral and Svidrigailov is amoral; yet both are strangely personable and rational men. Moreover, these outsiders, each in his own novel, apparently contradicts the major ideas presented by their authors.

Beginning with the author's preface and continuing through all of *Les Misérables*, Hugo portrays crime as being a social ill. The injustices in society have made men into thieves and forced women into prostitution, and once they have fallen, society condemns them to stay forever in a world of darkness and dishonor. But Thénardier is different. He, and perhaps some of his comrades who are less clearly sketched, seems to choose his dishonest life and stick to it gladly in matters both

59

large and small, even when better ways are open to him. The fact is that Thénardier neither acts nor reacts as a "victim" of society. Instead he is a member—and a most resourceful one—of the professional organized underworld. Therefore, his activities and those of his cohorts introduce a new aspect to the problem of social evil.

Paul Savey-Casard writes in a chapter entitled "La criminalité des *Misérables*":

> A l'époque des *Misérables*, [Hugo] a constaté une plaie plus profonde qui est la formation d'une contre-société, celle des bas-fonds. Elle est un symptôme autrement dangereux et appelle plus encore une réforme sociale.[14]

and:

> La Société actuelle est donc si mal organisée qu'elle crée elle-même des malfaiteurs et qu'elle les rive à leur crime. Après avoir forgé des criminels d'occasion, elle en fait des récidivistes et parfois, mieux encore, des criminels "par profession." Le peuple des bas-fonds est son oeuvre. Cette fois, la misère en a assez de souffrir et de subir, elle se révolte et entre en combat. La Société a fait des "damnés"; cet enfer se soulève et menace, et, dans sa rébellion, il veut tout emporter, la Société et la civilisation.[15]

All this, of course, underlines the impact of the theme of "social damnation," but does not specifically illuminate Thénardier's complexity as a character. The key to his multi-faceted nature lies in the fact that we are dealing here with, in the words of Maria Ley-Deutsch, "un monstre complet," "une bête sauvage, horrible."[16] Not once does Thénardier experience the temptation of goodness, the inclination to trade dishonesty for honesty, the need to pity or help. He has a diabolical imagination, a genius for survival, and a vengeful nature:

[C]omme il avait en lui une profonde fournaise de haine, comme il était de ces gens qui se vengent perpétuellement, qui accusent tout ce qui passe devant eux de tout ce qui est tombé sur eux, et qui sont toujours prêts à jeter sur le premier venu, comme légitime grief, le total des déceptions, des banqueroutes et des calamités de leur vie, comme tout ce levain se soulevait en lui et lui buillonnait dans la bouche et dans les yeux, il était épouvantable. Malheur à qui passait sous sa fureur alors! (pp. 394-95)

Clearly, Thénardier is a form of evil incarnate—the absolute antithesis of Jean Valjean. As Ms. Ley-Deutsch phrased it, "Tous les deux sont aux extrémités de la misère: Valjean essaie de se retrouver en suivant le chemin du bien; Thénardier prend le chemin du mal."[17]

In *Crime and Punishment* Svidrigailov stands out as a man without a moral sense. True, his character is not clear. The ghost that haunts him, seemingly more to his diversion than to his remorse, as well as his final suicide, are never explained. Paradoxically, the clues to Svidrigailov's committing suicide, after a night during which his own demon caught up with him, are to be found in two scenes involving Raskolnikov, one with Svidrigailov himself, the other with the police inspector.

When Raskolnikov and Svidrigailov meet for the first time, Dostoevsky indicates that there exists a mysterious connection between them. As Svidrigailov is telling of his familiarity with ghosts, Raskolnikov blurts out:

"Why did I think that something of this kind had undoubtedly happened to you," said Raskolnikov suddenly, and at the same moment he was astonished at having said that. He was

61

greatly perturbed.

"So? You thought so?" asked Svidrigailov in surprise. "Is that possible? But didn't I say that there is something in common between us, eh?"

"You never said that!" answered Raskolnikov sharply and heatedly.

"Didn't I?"

"No!"

"I thought I had. A while ago, when I came in and saw you lying with your eyes closed and pretending to sleep, I immediately told myself: 'This is the very same man.'

"What is that: the very same? What are you talking about?" shouted Raskolnikov.

"What about? Really, I do not know. . . ." (Vol. V, p. 297)

The second scene is the brilliant demonstration of Porfiry Petrovich's "psychological method." With uncanny clairvoyance Porfiry foresees Raskolnikov's future and predicts to him that unless the young man confesses his crime and accepts the suffering inherent to the human condition, he will condemn himself to much worse than what Justice demands. Raskolnikov is of the kind who cannot run away from his conscience which will—no matter when or where—demand its due. Guilt, no matter how rationalized or suppressed, will finally imprison him in a universe so discolored and distasteful that suicide will appear as the only possible way out. The "new order" he sought would be death or, in Svidrigailov's words, "America," where one would inescapably follow the other. Thus, in spite of his apparent lack of concern with morality, Svidrigailov's example demonstrates to Raskolnikov and to the reader that there is no exception to the rule and that the "superman's" philosophy leads only to disaster.

The textual existence of Svidrigailov and Thénardier

expresses a profound and constant concern on the part of their authors: the presence and the power of Evil. Yet to note this concern for Evil by the authors does not in itself explain these characters whose actions, whose very being, seem to run counter to the philosophical postulates of the novels in which they appear.

Throughout Hugo's work the basic assumption is that man is by nature good, that it is society which drives him to evil. (In this respect it is significant that all of Valjean's crimes are crimes against property, or against the law that protects property, rather than sins against people.) Contrary to Savey-Casard's imputation that he is "created by" and "riveted to" a "counter-society," Hugo gives no indication that Thénardier is trapped in a criminal underclass. True, such a class is shown to exist, and Thénardier to be a member of it; but he has ample opportunity to escape—he is highly energetic, intelligent, and often acquires enough money to attempt a fresh start. Even if he were born into the criminal class, and we are given absolutely no indication that he was, he is presented as a man of sufficient fortitude and resourcefulness to escape from it. He has some education and a wife who loves him and who would support him in whatever path he followed. Thus, we can only conclude that Thénardier is evil because he *chooses* to be so and that he will remain so until the end of his life. In Hugo's words:

La misère morale de Thénardier, *ce bourgeois manqué*, était irrémédiable; il fut en Amérique ce qu'il était en Europe. . . . Avec l'argent de Marius, Thénardier se fit négrier. (p. 1475, our italics)

These final words seal Thénardier's condemnation. He now has the first requirement of being a bourgeois:

63

a considerable sum of money. To fulfill the second requirement he also should have, instead of his *misère morale*, a *richesse morale*, of which he is "irremediably" deprived. The syntactic unit *bourgeois manqué* is formed on the model of the French syntagm *garçon manqué* (tomboy), in which the pejorative connotation falls not on *garçon* but on *manqué*. Thus had Thénardier become a *real* bourgeois by adopting the values of the bourgeoisie—not only work and money, but also probity—he might have at last been redeemed. On the contrary, what takes place is an acceleration of evil. Whereas in Valjean's last moments there is an acceleration of saintliness, Thénardier in the end becomes a slave dealer, an ignominious trade that stands as the very symbol both of the rottenness of his soul as well as of the corruption of the bourgeois ideal.

It is our feeling that this surface inconsistency was required in order to retain the deeper logic of the drama. Thénardier's evilness highlights the goodness of Valjean. Had Thénardier simply chosen to become a good man, it would have undercut the power of the conversion of Valjean who was redeemed through an act of human kindness and who has to endure great sufferings in order to remain true to the dictates of his conscience. The logical contradiction between social determinism and individual choice is not resolved by this conversion. That through the Bishop's intercession Valjean chooses to become good, despite those forces of society which drove him toward evil, is no less a contradiction than that Thénardier chooses evil and sticks to it, despite his many social opportunities to be good. Yet these logical opposites compose a structural unity and give dramatic consistency to the story of *Les Misérables* as but one episode in the unending struggle between light and darkness.

In the case of *Crime and Punishment* the conflict is that between social determinism and personal agency, and between divine and satanic forces competing within each individual. In these terms, Svidrigailov's character is not so "illogical" as that of Thénardier. Though an evil man, he is far from being a common villain; indeed, his evil lies precisely in his denial of his generous impulses and in his cynical refusal to follow the inclinations of his conscience.

Yet these ambiguities will have their own dramatically consistent outcome. When Svidrigailov is faced with the fact that Dunya is forever lost to him, there arises the possibility of abandoning his old self—the Don Juan self that has failed him—and of starting again as a better man. But here the "villain" thinks not of a foreign land which is the material El Dorado that Thénardier envisioned,[18] but of a spiritual New World that creates men anew.[19] To be afforded this possibility, Svidrigailov should, in Porfiry's formula, first confess to his sins. Then repentence could lead to rebirth. The only alternative is suicide. Whether because Svidrigailov is too lucid to believe in his own regeneration or too tired to attempt it, he decides to pull the trigger and enter his very own "America."

The effects of Svidrigailov's death are manifold: it gives a forceful warning to Raskolnikov, and thus contributes to the resolution of the main story line; it frees Dunya of any further pursuit or unpleasantness and therefore allows the first subplot to end in a happy marriage; and finally, it shows that if one cannot change completely and repent as Jean Valjean and Raskolnikov have done, nor make a consistent career of evil as does Thénardier, then one can only do as Javert did!

After almost two decades of pursuit, Javert at last comes face to face with a Jean Valjean who, no longer wanting to run, is willing to be arrested. At the crowning of so much effort one would expect Javert to experience unmitigated triumph and elation, but: ". . . il y avait eu en lui quelque chose du loup qui ressaisit sa proie et du chien qui retrouve son maître."(p. 1344)

This ambivalence of feeling will lead to Javert's downfall. To remain a "tigre légal" he must take Valjean in. Unfortunately, for a man whose lifelong efforts have been devoted to acting out his role as a policeman, in the end he can no longer help admitting that there might be exceptions to the rules and that Valjean is "plus voisin de l'ange que de l'homme"(p. 1346). Faced with both a revelation that cancels out the whole meaning of his life, and a dilemma between old certainties and new truths, Javert finds his only answer in suicide.

The four characters, Thénardier and Svidrigailov and Javert and Porfiry, thus stand in a kind of "cross-parallel" relationship to each other.

Javert	*Porfiry*
A. Policeman who gets his man. →	A. Policeman who gets his man.
B. A pursuer frustrated by virtue.	C. Steadfast attitude toward evil.
Thénardier	*Svidrigailov*
C. Steadfast attitude toward evil.	B. A pursuer frustrated by virtue who commits suicide.
D. Evildoer with idea of going to America. →	D. Evildoer with idea of going to America.

The description and reassembling of these elements makes clearer not only the function of the problem of Evil in each of the novels, but also why Javert commits suicide while Pofiry, as humane as he is professional, does not, and why Thénardier actually *goes* to America while Svidrigailov only *says* he is going to America but instead, like Javert, takes his own life. In Javert's death, true virtue, embodied in Valjean, vanquishes the injustice of society, as embodied in Javert. Personal evil, as embodied in Thénardier, goes largely unexplained. Yet in *Crime and Punishment* this basic distinction between personal and social levels of action or principles does not exist. Good and evil both coexist and are personal. Thus, the active characteristics and the final "adventure" of both Javert *and* Thénardier are passed on, in Dostoevsky's novel, to Svidrigailov.

* * *

Further examination of the plot structures of *Les Misérables* and *Crime and Punishment* undoubtedly could reveal further similarities. Our purpose in this chapter has been only to show such parallels with sufficient clarity to make the following points.

First the novel by Hugo and the novel by Dostoevsky draw on basically similar elements for their plots. The sequence of events has been changed in places, details and incidents added or deleted, episodes stressed or suppressed, motives and meanings changed. Yet both novels still stand as variations on the same identifiable structure, developed out of the same fund of materials.

Secondly, we have sought to persuade that the major differences between the two novels—the stress on sociology in one and on psychology in the other, the differences of *durée*, the characterization of the hero, and the variations on the subplots—all are to be explained in terms of the differing purposes the two writers had set for themselves. Given their different tasks, the similarities and dissimilarities become almost predictable. In effect, we can imagine that if Dostoevsky had consciously tried to adapt *Les Misérables* to convey his own message, the result could not have been very different from the novel *Crime and Punishment* as we have it today.

RASKOLNIKOV'S DREAMS: THEIR FUNCTION
AND THEIR LITERARY SOURCES

> A sick man's dreams are often remarkable for their extraordinary clarity, their vividness and their extreme resemblance to reality. A scene may be composed of monstrous elements but the setting and the whole representation are nevertheless so plausible, the details so subtle and unexpected but so artistically in keeping with the whole picture that the dreamer could never invent them in his waking state, even if he were an artist like Pushkin or Turgenev. Such dreams, such morbid dreams, are for a long time remembered and always make a strong impression on a man's already disturbed and excited nerves.
>
> *Fyodor Dostoevsky*, Crime and Punishment

It would be dangerous to surmise, on the basis of the structural similarities between *Les Misérables* and *Crime and Punishment* which we have uncovered, that Dostoevsky simply borrowed and reworked the plot elements from the French novel. While such an impression seems basically correct, it can be regarded only as a starting point and not a conclusion. The literary relation between Hugo and Dostoevsky is too intricate to be fully explained by so general a formulation. Therefore an examination of specific passages appears to be the most appropriate approach at this point. In this and the next chapter we will attempt to shed light on this literary relationship by concentration on Raskolnikov's dreams.

In *Crime and Punishment* the psychological drama partially unfolds through a series of highly emotional

69

dreams. These dreams intensify the plot and provide it with an additional dimension, for they serve to unify seemingly unconnected occurrences, to give hints of events to come, and to stimulate certain characters into action. Through these dreams the reader, gaining insight into Raskolnikov's unconscious motivation, acquires a new understanding of him. Raskolnikov is distinctly separate from the other characters: he is the only one (with the exception of Svidrigailov) whose inner world is known, for only these two characters have dreams.

Our present purpose is:

1. to uncover some sources of a symbolism generally considered Dostoevskian *par excellence*;

2. to analyse the structural function of dreams;

3. to study the relationship between these sources and their function in the novel.

RASKOLNIKOV'S FIRST DREAM

The Killing of the Mare

The day before he axed open the skull of an old pawnbroker, "Raskolnikov dreamed a terrible dream." He dreamt that he was once more a child of seven on an outing with his father in the village where they used to live. Passing in front of a noisy tavern, they were arrested by the following scene: a decrepit old mare harnessed to "one of the huge drays" has to pull "at a gallop" not only the heavy cart but also some seven peasants who had loaded themselves onto it with "witticisms and roars of laughter." Since the mare, "far from galloping . . . could barely stir at all," the joke rapidly degenerates. The nag's ribs are lashed with whips, its back is beaten with "a thick wooden shaft," and it is

70

finished off finally by its driver, Mikolka, with an "iron crowbar," much to the delight of most of the onlookers. But this display of rustic fun has quite another effect on the child who, choking with horror, sobs: "Papa, why did they . . . kill . . . the poor horse?"(Vol. V, p. 64). At this point, Raskolnikov "struggled for breath, tried to cry out, and awoke"(Vol. V, p. 65).

Our immediate interest does not lie in interpreting this dream but in investigating the possible literary sources Dostoevsky might have used in creating so striking and savage a scene. Three such sources may be: an apparently "autobiographical" reference that can be traced in Dostoevsky's own writing, an apparently parallel scene in "About the Weather" by the Russian poet Nekrasov, and the poem "Melancholia" by Victor Hugo.

Dostoevsky's Diary of a Writer

This first apparently autobiographical source can be found in Dostoevsky's *Diary of a Writer* for January 1876, in the third chapter, whose title reads in part, "Russian Society for the Protection of Animals" [Rossiskoye obshchestvo pokrovitelstva zhivotnym]. In this entry Dostoevsky recollects a brutal incident dealing with horses and carters that he saw during a trip from Moscow to St. Petersburg at the age of fifteen:

The posting station was directly opposite the inn, on the other side of the street. Suddenly a troika with a courier raced up to the porch. . . . [The courier] ran into the station house and probably "downed" a glass of vodka there. I remember my driver telling me at the time that couriers like that always drink a glass at each station, otherwise they would not stand "the ordeal." In the meantime a dashing new troika—to replace the old one—drew up at the posting station, and the driver, a youth of about 20, holding his greatcoat in his hands, and wearing a red shirt, jumped up onto the seat. The courier immediately raced out, dashed down the steps and sat in the back. The driver started off, but no sooner had he done so than the courier stood up and silently, without any words, raised his huge right fist and, from above, hit the back of the driver's head as hard as he could. He jerked forward, raised his whip and with all his might lashed at the middle horse. The horses leapt forward, but this did not appease the courier. There was method in this. It was not irritation but something premeditated and tested by many years of experience, and the terrible fist rose up again, and again struck the man in the back of his neck. This happened again and again, and went on until the troika was hidden from view. Needless to say, the driver, who could scarcely stand because of these blows, constantly and every second whipped his horses, as though he had taken leave of his senses and at last he whipped them so much that they raced forward as if possessed. Our driver explained to me that all the other couriers did almost the same, but that this one particularly so, and that they knew him. . . .

This disgusting scene remained in my mind forever. I was never able to forget [it]. . . . This scene appeared, as it were, as an emblem, as something which showed extremely vividly the connection of cause and effect. Here every blow aimed at the animal leapt, as it were, from every blow aimed at the man. At the end of the 40s, in the period of my most selfless and passionate dreams, I once suddenly had the idea that if I should ever found a philanthropic society I would certainly have this courier's troika engraved on its seal, as an emblem and a token [of its purpose].

Oh, no doubt, this is not 40 years ago and couriers do not beat the simple people but the simple people already beats itself, having retained the birch in its courts. But this is not the point, it is a matter of the causes that bring about the consequences. There are no more couriers, but there is still "firewater. . . ."[1]

Yet if we consider this passage from the *Diary* as a key to Rasolnikov's dream, it leaves much to be desired. In his book on Dostoevsky, William Woodin Rowe takes this whole passage at face value and states that it "reveals the dream to be strikingly autobiographical."[2] Such a statement would require, it seems, further documentation. It is true that parallels can be found between the dream scene and the *Diary*—such as drinking in an inn, pathological need for violence, and the presence of a childish bystander. There are indeed horses in both cases, but there is hardly anything in common between "the wretched old nag" which dies under an avalanche of blows and a *troika* which, under the whip, "races" at top speed, "as if possessed." Moreover, the real victim in the *Diary* account is obviously the driver, who is hit on the back of his head by the courier, much more than the horses. One should keep in mind that, as Ronald Hingley phrased it, "*The Diary of a Writer* is a diary only in name. It offers not a record of daily events, but a series of tirades often (though not always) sparked off by the events of the month in which a given chapter is being written."[3]

In this particular instance, Dostoevsky's "tirade" is triggered by an article he had recently read "about the solemn celebration of the tenth anniversary of the Russian Society for the Protection of Animals," and the point of his entry is to rail against "firewater," which causes people's inhumanity to their fellows as well as their barbaric treatment of animals.[4]

One should also remember that *The Diary of a Writer* started ten years after *Crime and Punishment*, and therefore if parallels and influences are to be considered, we ought to reverse the order suggested by Rowe and neither neglect nor exclude the influence of Dostoevsky's

73

fiction upon Dostoevsky or, in other words, the recurrence of themes, preoccupations and even of verbal echoes—all forming a substratum upon which the writer's creativity feeds itself.

Finally, even without *The Diary of a Writer* account, there is little doubt that Dostoevsky saw sights such as couriers madly lashing their drivers, for these were common enough. Apparently the reappearance of such a scene in the *Diary* was shaped by Dostoevsky's experience, by his own writing as well as by the standard fictional image of the courier in a European literature concerned with exposing the exploitation of the helpless.

In sum, then, we might look upon the *Diary* for 1876 as proof of Dostoevsky's immersement in contemporary affairs and of his concern for animal suffering, but as an inadequate explanation of how and why Raskolnikov came to dream such a dream.

Nekrasov's "About the Weather"

Another possible "Russian" source, and one which fits chronologically, is a famous poem by Nikolai Nekrasov entitled "About the Weather" ("O pogode," dated 1858-59), a part of which deals with the beating of a horse by its carter. In fact, tracing of the beating of the mare to Nekrasov has been suggested by Dostoevsky himself. In Chapter IV of the second part of *The Brothers Karamazov*, Ivan Karamazov expresses the thought that "We [Russian People] take a historical, spontaneous and intimate delight from torture by beating. There are some verses of Nekrasov about how a peasant whips a horse on the eyes, 'on its meek eyes.' Who has

74

not seen it? It is typically Russian"(Vol. IX, p. 302).

In his poem, Nekrasov describes a "hideously thin horse" which, unable to manage too heavy a load, is beaten by its carter first with a whip and then with a log. Blows fall on the back, the shoulders, and "the meek and weeping eyes" of the animal. The scene amuses the "idle passersby," among whom stands the poet, who watches with feelings of anger and helplessness. Finally, the driver's efforts are rewarded, for the beast succeeds in moving on, while the blows continue to rain.

In comparing Nekrasov's and Dostoevsky's texts, we note that in each there is:

1. The savage beating of an overloaded horse by its carter;

2. A specific identical detail: " 'Hit her on the nose and across the eyes, beat her across the eyes!' yelled Mikolka." "Again he [Nekrasov's carter] hits it . . . on the shoulders and on its meek and weeping eyes";

3. A crowd of merry onlookers with special emphasis on the reactions of one particular character; and

4. The animal's pathetic efforts to stir.

In the light of these parallels, are we to assume that Dostoevsky merely lifted Nekrasov's poem for *Crime and Punishment* and later used Ivan Karamazov to acknowledge his borrowing of narrative elements? Before making such an assertion, it would seem advisable to examine the points of *dis*similarity between Nekrasov's and Dostoevsky's texts.

1. *The Fate of the Horse:* In *Crime and Punishment*, the horse dies, whereas at the end of "About the Weather" it moves off ". . . at a quick and nervous pace";

2. *The Attitude of the Carter:* Nekrasov's carter is

a brute who mercilessly beats his horse with the purpose of making it pull an enormous load. The man is obviously cruel but he also is, in his own way, efficient, and he gets the job done by means of brutality. Dostoevsky's carter, on the other hand, is "roaring drunk" and "in a passion of anger." Rather than being brutally efficient, he does not believe his mare is capable of pulling her load in the first place. In fact, it appears that Mikolka stages a situation which will allow him to do what he wishes, which is to torture and ultimately kill his horse. This intent is made clear from the beginning of the scene, as Mikolka invites his drinking partners to partake in the action.

> "And as for this old mare, brothers, she's just breaking my heart. I can kill her for ought I care. . . . Get in, I tell you! I'll make her gallop. She'll gallop, all right." And he took up the whip delighting in the thought of beating the old nag. (Vol. V, p. 61)

When the mare finally gives up the ghost, Mikolka is "sorry that there was no longer anything to beat." It is clear, then, that the fate of the horse and the attitude of the carter in the respective texts are distinctly different.

3. *The Witness and his Role:* We know that Nekrasov's witness is the poet himself, whereas Dostoevsky's is a boy of seven. The poet assuages his "anger" at what he sees with a mixture of bitterness and sarcasm: "Shouldn't I intercede for it? It is the fashion to show pity in our age. . . . But we cannot help [even] ourselves!" On the other hand the child Raskolnikov has vainly tried to interfere. Throughout the beating he has been running around, "weeping . . . wringing his hands and crying aloud." The compassion and anguish are such

76

that when "one of the whips stung his face . . . he did not feel it." The poet marks the distance between "it" and "ourselves"—between animal and human—and rationalizes his decision not to intercede. But the little boy impulsively sides with the mare, shares its sufferings, and is "beside himself with pity and despair." Clearly, the fatalistic disengagement of the poet is in no way analogous to the horrified involvement of the child. The two are both cast in the role of witness, but the way in which each performs that role could hardly be more different.

In the light of these differences, can we still regard Nekrasov's poem as the source of the basic materials used by Dostoevsky? Since determining what went into Dostoevsky's writing is far from being a straightforward matter, we will say that although "About the Weather" could not convincingly be called *the* source, it is most likely *a* source among others. However, the similarities between the two texts are considerably outweighed by differences in structure and artistic presentation, and therefore our search should not end there.

Hugo's "Melancholia"

Perhaps a more satisfying clue to Dostoevsky's source for Raskolnikov's first dream will be found elsewhere. For this we must turn toward Victor Hugo, whose poem "Melancholia" was published in April 1856, and thus predating Nekrasov's poem by some three years, and *Crime and Punishment* by ten years.

The link between "Melancholia" and Raskolnikov's dream has been suggested as early as 1923 by I.I. Lapshin in *Dostoevsky's Aesthetics [Estetika Dostoevskogo]*.

Studying Dostoevsky's use of symbolic imagery, Lapshin notices that:

[Raskolnikov's] strange dream . . . shows an extraordinary development of a theme indicated by Hugo: both authors show a drunk carter who, having excessively overloaded his cart, savagely beats the harnessed jade and, seeing that she cannot carry the load, reaches a state of frenzy and kills her.[5]

Our interest in the murder of the mare in Raskolnikov's dream has provided us with three mistreated horses—Hugo's, Nekrasov's, and Dostoevsky's. The question now remains as to whether we shall let them go their separate ways or whether we can team them up together? If so, which horse do we harness first in this pitiful troika? In order to choose as accurately as possible, we shall try to establish that the three beasts all come from the same stable and that their deaths (when they occur in Hugo's and Dostoevsky's works) serve a similar symbolic function.

Given the firm chronology and the similarities that Lapshin noticed, there emerge amóng these texts, four possible relationships that deserve our attention. These may be diagrammed as follows:

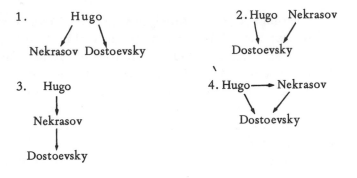

78

The external evidence already cited enables us to exclude pattern 1 in that it assumes Nekrasov had no influence on Dostoevsky. In the other patterns, however, the hypothesized relation between Hugo and Nekrasov obviously must be clarified. In light of external evidence alone, was such a relationship possible in the first place?

In his book on Nekrasov, Charles Corbet, discussing the merits of "About the Weather" says: "Ces visions sont si rapides, si nettement croquées en un clin d'oeil, que le lecteur moderne songe au cinéma."[6] The commentary proceeds, somewhat reluctantly, as follows: "Puis, défilent d'étranges scènes: par example, un cocher qui brutalise son cheval. *Le sujet avait—il été suggéré à Nekrasov par une traduction russe de "Melancholia"? La supposition est assez vraisemblable*"[7] (our italics). Corbet, one presumes, knows his Hugo well; nevertheless, he apparently regards this as an unimportant detail, for he immediately goes on to say:

> Dans ce cas, Nekrasov aurait égalé, sinon supassé son modèle. Nul n'a jamais pu lire ce passage sans éprouver un frisson dans le dos; *Dostoevskij en parle avec un sentiment d'horreur crispée. C'est le triomphe de l'art nekrasovien direct et brutal comme un coup de couteau.* On oublie les mots pour ne plus suivre que l'action: la littérature s'évanouit devant les choses. Hugo est plus rhéteur, plus poète en un sens, mais il émeut moins que Nekrasov qui évite d'expliquer, de commenter, et nous livre tout frémissante et nue l'horreur du spectacle. (Our italics, p. 273)

In sum, though literary indebtedness to Hugo is a "likely supposition," Corbet considers Nekrasov's mastery the only thing worth noticing and therefore decides against investigating sources. This dismissal notwithstanding,[8] we shall concentrate on the clues he ignored and explore further the likelikood that Nekrasov knew

79

and used Hugo's poem.

"Melancholia" and "About the Weather"

Victor Hugo, in the disguise of a workman, crossed the border into Belgium on December 11, 1851, exactly six days after the prince whom he labeled *Napoleon le Petit* betrayed the Constitution of 1848. Forty-eight years old, member of the Legislative Assembly, Peer of France, member of the French Academy, head of the French Romantic School since 1830, and a poet of international fame, Victor Hugo was on his way to nineteen years of self-imposed political exile. During these years, from 1851 to 1870, all that was liberal in the Western World—including Russia and the United States— saw in him a "Witness of the Light,"[9] the embodiment of Republican virtues and a prophet of the written word.

Les Châtiments (1853), Hugo's first collection of poems to be written in exile, was suffused with a politically inspired hatred for Napoleon III. Banned by the French censors, the book was published abroad[10] and for many years had to be smuggled into France.[11] No wonder his next collection, *Les Contemplations*— authorized for French publication, for it was to be of a purely lyrical nature—was eagerly awaited and became an immediate popular success.[12]

As for the possible interest of the Russian public in this particular work and the hypothesis that the intelligentsia were soon acquainted with it, it should suffice to remember that, in the words of M.P. Alekseyev:

In general the daily Russian press paid close attention to Victor Hugo; one could find in publications of the most divergent

80

views, anecdotes about Hugo, conversations that some resource-ful correspondent had had with him, and translations of his speeches. The newspapers published by Hugo and his family also reached Russia—they were brought here by Russians who visited Paris and they circulated, not entirely legally, among the reading public.[13]

Before *Les Contemplations* came out in Paris (on April 23, 1856), the readers of *The Fatherland Notes (Otechestvennye zapiski)* were alerted to the forthcoming publication:

Le Contemplations will appear tomorrow or the day after to-morrow and the whole of Paris awaits its appearance with avid impatience.[14]

In the section entitled "News from Abroad" ("Zag-ranichnye izvestiya") of *The Contemporary (Sovremennik)*, Number 6 for 1856, six enthusiastic pages were de-voted to Victor Hugo's new book:

One of the wonderful events in French literature is the publica-tion of Victor Hugo's *Les Contemplations*. (p. 214)

An accurate and thorough discussion of the book's divi-sions and content then follows, with emphasis on Hugo's system of ethics. The reviewer underlines Hugo's "poetical enthusiasm" for topics not traditionally thought of as poetic, and illustrates his comments with long excerpts from Hugo's poems. At one point he states that:

One of the best poems in this book is called "Melancholia." The poet examines social defects and human passions and sinks into a profound melancholy. (p. 217)

81

The reviewer closes with a few words about the reception given in France to *Les Contemplations*:

In Hugo, the enthusiastic journalist finds the heroic nature of Corneille, the mildness of Virgil, the charm of Aristophanes, the receptiveness of Juvenal. In his opinion we have here Dante and Béranger combined. Although we are far from taking such a panegyric as a serious appraisal of the works of Hugo, nonetheless the very success of the publication of this new book is sufficient proof that Hugo still has many ardent admirers. (p. 219)

Now, how likely is it that Nekrasov was acquainted with this literary news? The question appears almost superfluous for, aside from the fact that these two journals were for decades *the* leading literary periodicals, Nekrasov was, from 1846 to 1866, the proprietor and chief editor of *The Contemporary*. There is therefore little risk in assuming that he did read the review printed in his own journal, and it seems highly likely that he then went on to read the volume when texts finally made their way to Russia.[15]

The possibility of a literary relationship between Hugo and Nekrasov is the subject of a scholarly article published a decade ago in the Soviet Union. I.Z. Serman, in his paper of 1966 on "Nekrasov and Victor Hugo,"[16] focuses on the publication of *Les Contemplations*, on the reception of the book in Russia, and on the obvious fact that Hugo's social and "democratic" themes were of interest to Nekrasov. About one of the poems which had been singled out by *The Contemporary* reviewer, Serman writes that "the simple enumeration of the various themes of Hugo's 'Melancholia' forces one to remember Nekrasov's urban cycles such as "About the Weather."[17]

After naming some of Nekrasov's poems for which
"Melancholia" appears to be a likely source,[18] Serman
arrives at the main point of his research and states that:

> In Nekrasov's poem, "Before Dusk," from the cycle "About
> the Weather," the second part depicts the ugly scene of the beat-
> ing of a horse which is close to an identical scene in Hugo's "Mel-
> ancholia."
>
> In all examples so far, it has been possible to speak of a sim-
> ilarity in content and theme, and of the influence of certain
> images of Victor Hugo; but here *we have the case*—very rare in
> Nekrasov's work—*of an obvious translation* of a poem of Hugo,
> and a rather close one at that. (Our italics) (p. 133)

In order to be able to agree or disagree with
Serman, let us now submit these two poems to our
own scrutiny.

The vast collection of poems gathered under the
general title, *Les Contemplations*, is divided into six
books. In Book III, entitled *Les luttes et les rêves*, the
second poem is "Melancholia." Written in alexandrines,
"Melancholia" is a long narrative built on the central
themes of social inequities and the struggle between
Evil and the Christian ideals of charity and compassion.
The poem is divided into irregular stanzas, each a vi-
gnette illustrating some social abuse as, for example, the
seventeen-year-old seamstress forced into prostitution
by cold and hunger, children working fifteen hours a
day in factories, the well-fed and unscrupulous juror
sending to forced labor the man who stole a loaf of
bread. The sixth of these vignettes describes the killing
of a "trembling, haggard, lame" horse by a drunken
carter.

Written in iambic tetrameter, "About the Weather"
presents a series of gruesome vignettes of the streets of

St. Petersburg observed at different times of the day. The long narrative is divided into three parts respectively titled "Morning Walk" ("Utrennyaya progulka"), "Before Dusk" ("Do sumeryek"), and "Dusk" ("Sumerki"). The poet spends his "Morning Walk" helping an old woman lower a destitute civil servant into his grave which is, like the rest of the city, half flooded by uninterrupted rains. In "Before Dusk" the poet observes the evil effects of the surroundings—the rain is by then turning into snow—on different passersby. "Dusk" and fog bring on thoughts about the "miserable children" of the city who will never know the meaning of childhood. "Before Dusk" is internally divided into six independent parts, the second of which deals with the "cruel" beating of a "jaded" horse.

Let us now put side by side the two stanzas under consideration and see for ourselves to what extent Nekrasov's poem does in fact appear to be an "obvious translation" from Hugo and to what extent it is his own.

Melancholia

1 Le pesant chariot porte une énorme pierre;
2 Le limonier, suant du mors à la croupière,
3 Tire, et le roulier fouette, et le pavé glissant
4 Monte, et le cheval triste a le poitrail en sang.
5 Il tire, traîne, geint, tire encore, et s'arrête.
6 Le fouet noir tourbillonne au-dessus de sa tête;
7 C'est lundi; l'homme hier buvait aux Porcherons
8 Un vin plein de fureur, de cris et de jurons;
9 Oh! quelle est donc la loi formidable qui livre
10 L'être à l'être, et la bête effarée à l'homme ivre?
11 L'animal éperdu ne peut plus faire un pas;
12 Il sent l'ombre sur lui peser; il ne sait pas,
13 Sous le bloc qui l'écrase et le fouet qui l'assomme,

14 Ce que lui veut la pierre et ce que lui veut l'homme.
15 Et le roulier n'est plus qu'un orage de coups
16 Tombant sur ce forçat qui traîne des licous,
17 Qui souffre, et ne connait ni repos ni dimanche.
18 Si la corde se casse, il frappe avec le manche,
19 Et, si le fouet se casse, il frappe avec le pied;
20 Et le cheval, tremblant, hagard, estropié,
21 Baisse son cou lugubre et sa tête égarée:
22 On entend, sous les coups de la botte ferrée,
23 Sonner le ventre nu du pauvre être muet;
24 Il râle; tout à l'heure encore il remuait,
25 Mais il ne bouge plus et sa force est finie.
26 Et les coups furieux pleuvent; son agonie
27 Tente un dernier effort; son pied fait un écart,
28 Il tombe, et le voilà brisé sous le brancard;
29 Et, dans l'ombre, pendant que son bourreau redouble,
30 Il regarde Quelqu'un de sa prunelle trouble;
31 Et l'on voit lentement s'éteindre, humble et terni,
32 Son oeil plein des stupeurs sombres de l'infini
33 Où luit vaguement l'âme effrayante des choses.
34 Hélas![19]

Before Dusk

1 Under the cruel hand of a man,
2 Scarcely alive, hideously thin,
3 A jaded horse strains at every nerve
4 Dragging a load too heavy for it.
5 Now it staggers and stops
6 Get along! says the driver seizing a log
7 (He thought the whip was not enough)
8 And beat it, beat it for all he was worth!
9 Putting its legs somehow wide apart,
10 Steaming, falling to its hind legs,
11 The horse only sighed deeply
12 And looked (as people do

13 Submitting to unjust attacks).
14 Again he hits it: on the back and flanks,
15 And running in front, on the shoulders
16 And on its meek and weeping eyes!
17 All in vain. The nag stood
18 Covered with stripes from the whip,
19 Answering each blow
20 With a steady movement of its tail.
21 This amused the idle passersby
22 Each of them put in his word,
23 I was angry and thought gloomily:
24 "Shouldn't I intercede for it?
25 It is the fashion to show pity in our age,
26 We would even be glad to help you,
27 Dumb victim of the people,
28 But we cannot help ourselves!"
29 The driver had not labored in vain:
30 At last he got what he wanted!
31 But the last scene was
32 More revolting to behold than the first:
33 The horse suddenly strained and moved off
34 Somehow sideways, at a quick and nervous pace,
35 And the driver at every step,
36 In gratitude for these efforts
37 Belabored its flanks with his whip
38 And himself ran along beside.[20]

When examining the structural progression of each poem, we find the following divisions:
In Nekrasov,
    A. Lines 1-20
        Savage beating of a horse by its carter.
    B. Lines 21-28
        Reactions of people witnessing the scene, including the poet.
    C. Lines 29-38

"Disgusting result" of the man's savagery: the horse moves forward "rewarded"
by more uninterrupted blows.
  In Hugo,
    A. Lines 1-25
      Savage beating of a horse by his drunken
      carter.
    B. Lines 26-28
      The horse falls and breaks his back.
    C. Lines 29-34
      Death of the horse. The poet uses reli-
      gious symbolism to show the soul free-
      ing itself from the matter.
  These parallels and the distinctions in structure
show clearly that Part A of "Before Dusk" indeed can
be read, if not as a literal translation of Part A of "Melancholia," at least as a very close adaptation of it. Yet
Nekrasov's omission of Hugo's seventh and eighth lines—
the drunkenness motif—and his reduction of personification devices show the difference of his intent. No matter how cruelly treated, his "jaded horse" remains "a
nag/Answering each blow/With a steady movement of
its tail," (lines 17, 19, and 20). The adjectives used for
the animal are rather neutral and expectable within the
context:
    2 scarcely alive, hideously thin
    3 crippled horse
    16 meek and weeping eyes
    27 dumb victim
  What we have is a pathetic but quite straightforward picture of an animal abused by a man. Hugo's different intent is clear from the outset of his poem. In
"Melancholia" everything participates in a symbolic
drama. Even the wagon is invested with a life of its own

87

since, instead of being *loaded* with stones, it *carries (porte)* them. Another example of this animistic perspective is line 14 where Hugo humanizes even the stone by attributing to it a will as autonomous as that of a man *(Ce que lui veut la pierre et ce que lui veut l'homme)*.

At first neither man nor animal are identified by the generic names which would separate them. Rather, in being characterized by their functions—*le limonier* and *le roulier*—they are put on an equal footing as participants in the common effort. Then, as the man becomes more beastly, the humanness of the horse increases. This is made even clearer when we consider the vocabulary used to describe the horse's ordeal. The epithets chosen do not pertain, as a matter of course, to the horse's animal nature, but instead underline its human aspect as victim.

  4 Cheval triste
10 bête effarée
11 animal éperdu
20 le cheval, tremblant, hagard, estropié
21 cou lugubre . . . tête égarée
23 pauvre être muet

Exhaustion and bewilderment (as depicted in lines 11-14) are stated in psychological terms of "feeling" and "knowing" (il *sent* . . . *il ne sait* pas) and could apply to any "being" in an identical situation. Such a being could, for instance, be a "forçat . . . Qui souffre, et ne connaît ni repos ni dimanche."

What emerges here is not the basic antithesis of man versus animal, but *rather* the parallel contrast of slave versus master *(pauvre être muet—botte ferrée)*, which is carried to its ultimate stage of condemned versus executioner *(Il râle . . . son agonie—son bourreau)*. It is to this problem of evil and injustice that Hugo refers when asking, "Oh! quelle est donc la loi formidable qui livre/L'être à l'être, et la bête effarée à l'homme ivre?" (lines 9 and 10). In asking this question, Hugo enlarges the scope of the beating, gives it an awesome and timeless quality, and thus elevates the drama to a metaphysical level.[21] In sum, the contents of Parts A allow rather close parallels, but one cannot ignore the striking differences of style and intent of Nekrasov and Hugo.

As for the content of Parts B, they differ drastically. "Before Dusk" provides the amusement of the "idle passersby" and an actual witness—the poet—who comments on the scene. Part B of "Melancholia" shows' the animal in agony, with its back broken. It is short, only three lines, and serves as a transition between the end of the physical action and the unexpected concluding statements.

Parts C also differ completely in the two poems, since Nekrasov's horse survives and carries on, while Hugo's dies. In regard to Nekrasov's original ending, Serman observes:

> I don't believe that the theme of this poem could be interpreted allegorically, but against the background of Hugo's poem, which is suffused with religious symbolism, the optimistic ending of Nekrasov's poem can be interpreted not only in a realistic and topical sense, but in a figurative, social and historical sense.[22]

It would be difficult to disagree with this assessment. Indeed, the last four lines of "Melancholia" reflect not only the poet's pity for the animal and his certitude that God is omnipresent and omniscient, but also his belief that life in matter is an inherent part of the cosmological life. The end of the poem shows Hugo's reflection on the problem of Evil, and his conception of cosmic forces in action as illustrated by the antithesis of shadows and light (ombre-luit). By now the horse has become a metaphor, conveying the poet's belief in the salvation of the soul.

It should now be clear that Nekrasov was influenced by the horse episode in "Melancholia" and integrated it into his own work. In terms of the diagrams presented earlier with reference to influences on Dostoevsky, this would eliminate the possibility of pattern 2, which assumes there was no relation between Hugo and Nekrasov. However, this still leaves the possibilities of patterns 3 and 4.

The Troika Reharnessed

Nekrasov, while borrowing from Hugo, also changed a number of elements, as can be seen by isolating the items exclusive to only one of the two poems:

Melancholia	Before Dusk
Drunkenness of the carter	Meek eyes
Death of the horse	Jeering crowd
Religious symbolism	Poet as witness
Metaphysical overtones	Social symbolism
	Historical overtones

This listing shows that Raskolnikov's dream about the killing of the mare is, in major respects, closer to "Melancholia" than to "Before Dusk." It turns out that when Dostoevsky used material from Nekrasov, Ivan Karamazov told us quite accurately what it amounted to: "There are lines in Nekrasov about how a peasant

90

whips a horse on the eyes, 'on its meek eyes'." The lashing on the eyes and the presence of a crowd are the only two descriptive details common to both Dostoevsky and Nekrasov, but not found in "Melancholia," which provided us with the original beating, agony, and death of the animal.

Let us summarize by presenting the following formula:

$$\text{Hugo's} \left\{ \begin{matrix} A \\ B \\ C \end{matrix} \right. + \text{Nekrasov's} \left\{ \begin{matrix} A \\ B \end{matrix} \right. \text{yield} \quad \begin{matrix} \text{the majority of fac-} \\ \text{tual elements incor-} \\ \text{porated by Dostoev-} \\ \text{sky in Raskolnikov's} \\ \text{first dream.} \end{matrix}$$

What becomes clear is that the strident aspect of the inhumanity of Hugo's carter and the symbolic humanizing of the animal and its sufferings have found their way into the "murder" scene of Raskolnikov's dream and have helped to create a "Russian" tone. However, Dostoevsky could not have absorbed these elements of Hugo's poem through Nekrasov, who had not incorporated them into "Before Dusk."

We thus can see that the relationship between sources, at this point, seems most accurately illustrated by our pattern 4. Indeed, such a diagram suggests not only the independent influence of both Hugo and Dostoevsky (pattern 2), but also the handing down of partial material from Hugo *through* Nekrasov (pattern 3), as well as Nekrasov's own literary indebtedness to Hugo.

As striking as such differences and similarities appear, attribution of influence still might not be wholly convincing. There is, however, another piece of evidence of a Hugo-Dostoevsky relationship. We shall now turn to *Les Misérables*.

Where a Fourth Horse Appears

Algernon Charles Swinburne, in his monograph of 1866 on Hugo, whom he called "the greatest poet of this century," observed that:

. . . the noble poem called "Melancholia" has in it a foretaste and a promise of all the passionate meditation, all the studious and indefatigable pity, all the forces of wisdom and of mercy which were to find their completer and supreme expression in *Les Misérables*.[23]

If the mention of *Les Misérables* evokes the victimizing of the poor and the ruthless inequities of a blind judicial system, it does not always bring to mind the merciless killing of a horse. It will be useful, nonetheless, to consider the following excerpt from the chapter in *Les Misérables* entitled "Mort d'un Cheval":

Tholomyès, lancé, se serait difficilement arrêté, si un cheval ne se fût abattu sur le quai en cet instant-là même. Du choc, la charrette et l'orateur restèrent courts. C'était une jument beauceronne, vieille et maigre et digne de l'équarrisseur, qui traînait une charrette fort lourde. Parvenue devant Bombarda, la bête, épuisée et accablée, avait refusé d'aller plus loin. Cet incident avait fait de la foule. A peine le charretier, jurant et indigné, avait-il eu le temps de prononcer avec l'énergie convenable le mot sacramentel: *mâtin!* appuyé d'un implacable coup de fouet, que la haridelle était tombée pour ne plus se relever. Au brouhaha des passants, les gais auditeurs de Tholomyès tournèrent la tête, et Tholomyès en profita pour clore son allocution par cette strophe mélancolique:

92

Elle était de ce monde ou coucous et carrosses
    Ont le même destin,
Et, rosse, elle a vécu ce que vivent les rosses,
    L'espace d'un: mâtin![24]

—Pauvre cheval, soupira Fantine.
Et Dahlia s'écria:
—Voila Fantine qui va se mettre à plaindre les chevaux! Peut-on être fichue bête comme ça! (p. 148)

The basic action material in this passage from *Les Misérables* presents an obvious similarity to "Melancholia." Even more remarkably from our point of view, it displays some striking similarities to Raskolnikov's dream. The scene takes place in front of a popular inn: an old mare is forced to carry an impossible load; the carter kills the exhausted beast with a pitiless cut from the whip; there is a crowd and there is noise; and above all there is a sympathetic witness in the person of a young woman named Fantine. One might wonder what is the meaning of this scene in *Les Misérables*? What is really happening or about to happen at Bombarda's?

"Quant à Fantine, c'était la joie"

She was 18 years old, "a lovely blonde with fine teeth" who worked for her living. She loved the 30-year-old "student" Tholomyès and he was "her first love." One day, after some two years of happiness, Tholomyès suggests to three of his friends (whose "favorites" are Fantine's friends) to treat the ladies to a joint surprise. "A dazzling pleasure party" takes place on the following Sunday. After spending the day in the country the party goes to the cabaret Bombarda, on the Champs Elysées, for a dinner, to be followed by the promised surprise. When the moment arrives, the four gentlemen depart and promptly hop the stagecoach for Toulouse. One hour later, according to instructions, the surprise in the form of a letter is brought in to the four girls. It reads as follows:

A l'heure où vous lirez ceci, cinq chevaux fougueux nous rapporteront à nos papas et à nos mamans. Nous fichons le camp, comme dit Bossuet. Nous partons, nous sommes partis. . . . Pleurez-nous rapidement et remplacez-nous vite. Si cette lettre vous déchire, rendez-le-lui. Adieu. (p. 151)

Recovering quite promptly, the girls burst out laughing and prepare themselves for new adventures. But Fantine,

Une heure après, quand elle fut rentrée dans sa chambre, elle pleura. C'était, nous l'avons dit, son premier amour; elle s'était donnée à ce Tholomyès comme à un mari, et la pauvre fille avait un enfant. (p. 151)

Thus begins Fantine's irrevocable downfall.[25]

Turning back to the killing of the mare with "one pitiless cut of the whip" in front of the inn, it is significant that the incident takes place immediately *before* Tholomyès and his friends depart. In this context it appears as a symbolically transparent preparatory device to the fate of Fantine, who was called "une fichue bête" for wasting pity on a horse. In fact, it is her "execution" which has been planned, and the blow she is about to receive is as deadly as the one that just killed a mare.[26]

The following progression has emerged from our texts. "Melancholia" can be read as a metaphor in which

94

the murder of the horse is a crime against humanity in general. In *Les Misérables* the horse's falling and expiring functions as the "rehearsal" for a woman's fall and death; there is a symbolic link between the blows administered to an animal and the events that will bring down a human being—which is precisely what happens in *Crime and Punishment*. Raskolnikov, in his dream, pre-enacts the murder he is to carry out the next day. None of this is to be found in Nekrasov. The whole of "About the Weather" (including the horse's episode in "Before Dusk") is a depiction of the degrading effects of city life on poor folks. There does not appear to be any further or more complex meaning to this verse treatment of social humanitarianism.

Structural Function of Raskolnikov's Dream

In all the scenes studied, the horse is the embodiment of the Victim as an innocent and exploitable creature, deprived by its very nature and circumstances of the means of fighting back, and therefore doomed to destruction.

Hugo's use of the killing of a mare as a premonitory device to the fate of a woman can be found in Raskolnikov's dream, and we will consider it after addresssing the following questions: Why did Dostoevsky use a dream frame for the killing of the mare? Couldn't Raskolnikov actually see such a "typically Russian scene" on the street and be equally upset by the cruelty of the spectacle? The whole episode is indeed so remarkably lifelike, coherent, and accurate in its details that the reader might not guess that it is a dream had he not been told so.

95

It seems that these questions are relevant to our study, for they can be answered only if one considers the structural function and psychological implications of the dream scene. Raskolnikov's dream occurs at the beginning of the book (Chapter V) both literally and in terms of the actual time of the narrative. Two days have not yet elapsed since the story of Raskolnikov started for us, but they are two very full days indeed. The narrative has been moving at such great speed that in four relatively short chapters—and one and a half days[27]— we have learned about: (1) Raskolnikov's existence and circumstances of life; (2) his plan to murder an old pawnbroker; (3) his meeting with the wretched Marmeladov and his family, as well as the existence and occupation of Sonya Marmeladov who, although neither Raskolnikov nor the reader have yet met her, is already a subject of preoccupation to both; (4) Raskolnikov's mother and sister Dunya, their financial difficulties for the last year, and Dunya's recent betrothal to Peter Petrovich Luzhin; (5) Raskolnikov's reactions to this news, followed by his meeting on the street with a drunken girl and his erratic attempts to interfere; (6) Raskolnikov's having a fever, wandering aimlessly in the countryside, and collapsing into sleep behind some bushes by the side of the road.

In reflecting on the number and nature of these items, one realizes that Raskolnikov has been subjected to a bombardment of rather horrible news and sights. The aggregate impact of these calamities cries out to be given meaning, yet a rational explanation would have impeded the pace of the action and narrative. Instead, by using the dream symbolically, Dostoevsky is able to gather the seemingly unrelated threads of the story, show their significance for the hero, and accelerate the

96

denouement, i.e., Raskolnikov's determination to kill, which he will carry out the next day. Thus, Raskolnikov's murderous intentions, his worries about his family, and various events of which he recently was a part, all are catalyzed under the guise of "a childhood reminiscence."

It also can be seen that Dostoevsky perceived and understood intuitively what Sigmund Freud was later to investigate and explain scientifically. Raskolnikov's dream combines numerous elements and processes that are identified in Freudian theory and that would easily lend themselves to a psychoanalytic interpretation.[28]

Beyond creating dramatic conflict while at the same time affording psychological resolution, the dream also provides new biographical data about the dreamer. Different aspects of Raskolnikov's personality are brought out, and the built-in tensions of the dream illustrate the conflicts that rage between them. Whereas the detail, length, and unrelieved sadism of the action make the dream terrible, the internal conflicts of the dreamer make it terrifying.

The child Raskolnikov is seven, devout, church-loving and impressionable. He and his father are on their way to the cemetery. They pass in front of a tavern where Mikolka the drunken carter and his friends beat an overloaded mare to death with crowbars and whips. The child witnesses the unbearable scene in its entirety. When the animal finally dies, "the poor little boy was quite beside himself. He pushed his way, shrieking, through the crowd to the mare, put his arms around the dead, blood-stained muzzle and kissed its eyes and mouth. . . . Then he sprang up and rushed furiously at Mikolka with his fists clenched." (Vol. V, p. 64)

97

The child's identification with the slaughtered animal is made clear, as well as his hatred of the killer. But, in terms of the dream, who is this Mikolka? Ruth Mortimer points out that "Behind Mikolka's act of violence lies the larger design of Raskolnikov's intended murder of the old woman. In this context Mikolka is Raskolnikov himself, and the mare, his victim."[29] The fact that Mikolka is intended as another Raskolnikov is corroborated by the dreamer's words upon awakening: "Is it possible, is it possible, that *I* really shall take an axe and strike her on the head, smash open her skull. . . ." The dream's pitiless length and detail can be seen as correspondences of the split between the two components of Raskolnikov's nature—the sufferer and the potential murderer.

If the killing of the mare foreshadows the killing of the pawnbroker, the intensity and duration of the animal's struggle express another source of the dreamer's anxiety and another theme treated by Dostoevsky. The "preparatory" scene to this intense suffering in the dream is Raskolnikov's encounter, a few hours earlier, with a girl "of sixteen, or perhaps only fifteen or so," staggering down the street. Her strange behavior and torn and disarrayed clothing engage his attention. Looking more closely at her, he remarks that "she can hardly be a professional. More likely somebody made her drink and abused her." Raskolnikov's first impulse is to help the girl to get home and prevent her from being molested further. Soon, however, a "feeling of revulsion" overcomes him, his charitable interest wanes and he decides he has no business interfering.

This episode can be seen as another possible answer to why the mare sequence was put into a dream and not just encountered in the street. Here we have a closely comparable event, the coming face to face with injustice, that not only takes place in the street, but also ties in emotionally and structurally with further developments of the novel. The unfortunate girl liberates Raskolnikov's spontaneous, compassionate feelings, just as the mare did in the dream. But soon Raskolnikov's conscious (murderous) mind gains control and he makes statistical and dehumanizing remarks. In the dream the cynical consciousness is suspended and we see the child's natural response to brutality. Upon awakening, however, horror and pity are promptly checked and again the murderous mind takes over.

Thus the encounter with the girl functions as a premonitory device to Raskolnikov's rejection of the warning of the dream, and as an indicator of the degree of corrosion of his moral sensibility. These portrayals of Raskolnikov awake and asleep are moreover linked with the epilogue of the novel insofar as they offer an early glimpse into the "real" character of the hero—the innocent child, the compassionate young man—who will emerge fully only after he has sincerely atoned for his crime and accepted his punishment.

The episode with the girl also unlocks the meaning of the dream by showing the correspondence between the characters in the dream—particularly the mare—to those in Raskolnikov's waking life. Raskolnikov's ambivalence[30] toward the young girl stems from his concern and indignation for the fate of his sister who is about to "sell herself" by marrying the "practical and very busy" Luzhin. In his mind, Raskolnikov already has equated Dunya to Sonya. The first feels it is her duty to marry a forty-five-year-old man so that Raskolnikov's "happiness may be secured [and] he may be kept at the University"; the second prostitutes herself for the sake of her little brother and sisters.[31] This ambivalence is dwelt upon and stated explicitly in Raskolnikov's "mutterings to himself" after he has read his mother's letter:

Why, perhaps we would not refuse even Sonechka's fate. Sonechka, Sonechka Marmeladova, Sonechka the eternal, while the world lasts! . . . Do you know, Dunechka, that Sonechka's fate is no whit worse than yours with Mr. Luzhin? (Vol. V, p. 49)

While Raskolnikov tormented himself with such ideas, "his attention became fixed" on the girl. This meeting crystalizes these associations in Raskolnikov's mind just as a chemical solution draws the unseen image to the surface of the film. The drunken girl already is a Sonya, and Dunya is, in a way, a potential Sonya. To Raskolnikov, to await such a life of degradation is to be as an animal for hire—a mare, for example, which becomes "the property" of whoever buys her.[32] This is clearly shown in Raskolnikov's reflecting upon this encounter. "Poor girl!" he says,

When she comes to herself, there will be tears, and then her mother will get to know. . . . First she will get a thrashing, then she will be beaten with a whip, painfully and shamefully, and perhaps she will even be driven out. . . . And even if she isn't, the Darya Franzovnas[33] will get wind of her, and she will be hunted this way and that. . . . (Vol. V, p. 56)

Raskolnikov vacillates between Christian compassion for the girl and irritated rejection of the whole situation, but he can neither separate nor reconcile these contradictions: "Pah! Let her go! They say it must be so. Such and such a percentage, they say, must go every year. . . . And what if Dunechka is included in the percentage. . ."

These inconsistencies of thought will characterize Raskolnikov's attitude and behavior towards both his sister and Sonya throughout the novel. Thus in Raskolnikov's dream, which combines all these elements, the mare "will be beaten with a whip, painfully and shamefully," just as girls reduced to prostitution are beaten by life as Fantine was, and then killed as the old woman will be killed the next day. By the device of a dream,[34] then, the author is able to gather many episodes and characters and give a simultaneous insight into the past, present, and future of the novel's hero. Moreover, had Dostoevsky put forward the dream material as an incident observed in waking life, such an objective presentation would have robbed the incident of its tremendous power to synthesize Raskolnikov's subjective psychological state. Conversely, as a dream, the synthesis is uniquely a creation of the hero and, as such, is a pure symbolization of his personal construction of reality.

"Melancholia," Les Misérables and Crime and Punishment

If we return now to the problem of literary influence, we note from the above internal analyses that our previous hypothesis, pattern 4, is incomplete, for it fails to show the possibility of a relationship between Les Misérables and Crime and Punishment. The addition of this new element might be incorporated in the following manner (pattern 5):

101

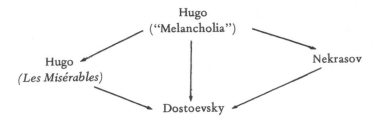

In the above diagram, we assume, of course, that Dostoevsky actually had read "Melancholia" as well as *Les Misérables*. Unless we can show that this did in fact occur, will we be unable to regard Hugo's works as primary literary sources—in the sense that there was not merely a parallel development, but that they provided real source material for *Crime and Punishment*?

From February 1854 to July 1859, Dostoevsky served as a private in the garrison town of Semipalatinsk. "Intellectually," writes E.H. Carr, "it was a change from darkness to faint twilight." Nevertheless, it afforded Dostoevsky some freedom to resume activities of which he had been deprived for so long—writing and reading. Of this period, he wrote:

> I remember that in Siberia, in 1854, when I came out of detention I began to read all the literature which had been written without me during five years.[35]

Dostoevsky's letters to his brother attest to his eclecticism and his avidity.[36] He enjoyed reading Gogol, Pushkin, and Victor Hugo[37] to his friend Baron Wrangel, the Districk Prosecutor of Semipalatinsk who, among many other precious qualities, had the ability to provide books, newspapers, and literary journals. Is it not likely that, though stationed far from Moscow near the Chinese border, Dostoevsky nevertheless came across reviews of

Hugo's new work? Furthermore, is it not probable that when he returned to St. Petersburg in 1859, he was able to read Hugo's text at some point before he started writing *Crime and Punishment*, that is, in 1865? The chances are excellent that he did, considering Hugo's popularity in Russia, Dostoevsky's general knowledge of contemporary literature, and his lifelong interest in other works of Hugo.

At this point it seems that we can safely conclude, on the strength of internal evidence, that Dostoevsky read "Melancholia," at least in *Les Contemplations*, and that he responded to the appearance in Hugo's poetry of a new quality of pity for animals and their senseless sufferings.[38]

As for *Les Misérables*, we know how Dostoevsky read the book as soon as it appeared in 1862 and subsequently reread it a number of times. We believe he had to react to and fully comprehend the use made of the death of the mare in the French novel, for it clearly answered his own vision, showing as it did aspects of Hugo's apprehension of the world for which the Russian writer felt remarkable affinities.

One may ask, finally, that if there is a case to be made for an influence of Hugo on Dostoevsky, why Ivan —who is so very "European"—does not cite Hugo's writing instead of Nekrasov's?

Let us first keep in mind that *The Brothers Karamazov* was published in 1879, and that Dostoevsky was unlikely to approve wholeheartedly of Hugo's political activities during the 70s. France's greatest poet had put an end to exile and returned to Paris on September 5, 1870, that is, after the fall of the Second Empire, and after the proclamation of the Third Republic. Hugo was to remain until the end of his life a staunch Republican,

103

often opposed—in the Senate, for example, of which he became a member in 1876—for his leftist and anti-clerical views.[39]

Secondly, since Ivan is discoursing about Russia observed from historical and national angles, and although those angles are most unflattering, there is an obvious need for a national example, and not a foreign one, to illustrate a "typically Russian" deed.[40] For all her defects, Russia is the motherland, and Ivan *is* a Russian. And what does being a Russian mean for Ivan?

> We [Russian people] take a historical, spontaneous and intimate delight in torture by beating. There are some verses of Nekrasov about how a peasant whips a horse on the eyes, "on its meek eyes." Who has not seen it? It is typically Russian. He describes how the puny horse, which has been given too much to carry, gets stuck with its cart and cannot move. *The peasant beats it, beats it savagely, beats it, in a word, not realizing what he is doing, whipping it painfully and innumerable times in the intoxication of beating: "Although you haven't the strength, get a move on, die, but get a move on!"* The little nag leaps forward, then he begins to whip it, the defenseless creature, on its crying "meek eyes." Beside itself, it pulls and gets the cart going, and moves off all trembling, not breathing, with a kind of sideways movement, tripping along, somehow unnaturally and shamefully —the way Nekrasov tells it it is terrifying. But it is only a horse after all, God himself has given horses to be whipped. (Our italics, Vol. IX, p. 302)

Interestingly enough, Ivan's reference to death, pain, the intoxication of beating, and God's will reminds us much less of Nekrasov's brutal street scene than of the savagery of "Melancholia," of *Les Misérables*, and of Raskolnikov's dream. In "Melancholia" the horse's death illustrates mankind's blind cruelty and man breaking the laws of the universe by defiling God's work. In *Les Misérables* the horse's death parallels the betrayal of a human being and illustrates the tortures inflicted by society upon its outcasts.

Dostoevsky, in focusing on these themes, has made them more explicit and has given them new psychological and emotional depths and complexity of meaning. The death of Mikolka's mare illustrates all together the fate of girls "who cannot earn fifteen kopeks a day," the murderous intent of Raskolnikov, and the struggle between the child of God and the rebel against God. Thus, through the magnifying glass of the dream, Dostoevsky has afforded his readers a simultaneous exploration of Raskolnikov's conscious and unconscious torments and motivations.

Therefore our contention is that Dostoevsky, having fully perceived and comprehended Hugo's message, artistically incorporated the horse's death to fulfill the intentions of his own novel.

"LA SOMBRE AVENTURE D'UNE AME MALADE"

Ce rêve, comme la plupart des rêves, ne se rapportait à la situation que par je ne sais quoi de funeste et de poignant, mais il lui fit impression.

Victor Hugo, Les Misérables

A Model Dream

Tormented by thoughts of crime and death, the hero fell asleep and began to dream.

Late at night, in a terribly familiar apartment, he had a strange and sinister feeling and then, in the stillness, heard noises which were frighteningly inappropriate for that time and place. He stood still and listened, but now it was quiet. He went into the living room and in the pale light everything took on an eerie cast—the furniture standing on the floor, the pictures hanging in their frames. Then he saw something dark in the corner between the wall and the cupboard, and thought that someone must be hiding there. He went over and, pulling back the cover, saw a frail old woman hiding by the cupboard. She was immobile and had a blank expression on her face. The hero assaulted her with sadistic brutality but she made no response. His fear turned to anger and he began attacking her once more. But again she showed no reaction, as though she were a piece of wood. Then suddenly and threateningly she came to life, as if his assault on her had been for naught.

Terrified, he woke up and someone was beside his bed.

RASKOLNIKOV'S THIRD DREAM[1]

Nightmare "à la russe"

Raskolnikov's third dream occurs a week after the double murder of the pawnbroker and her unfortunate sister Lizaveta. Neither the extraordinary tempo of the narrative nor the hero's frenzy and inner torments have relented. In some seven days, alternating between "mingled sleep and delirium," or wandering on the streets and making erratic social calls, Raskolnikov has aroused the suspicion of the police officer Porfiry Petrovich, suffered a brain fever, antagonized Luzhin, his brother-in-law to be, gone to a tavern where he made a "mad" confession to the police clerk Zametov, compulsively revisited the scene of the crime, witnessed Marmeladov's death under horses' hooves, met Sonya and given all his money to her consumptive stepmother, and bewildered and appalled his whole entourage—including his mother and sister Dunya, whom he had not seen in three years—by his physical collapse and pathological behavior.

Such extravagances, incoherences and contradictions point to the extreme need and the extreme fear—emblematic of the Dostoevskian character—both of losing and of maintaining contact with others. Steps toward contact (aborted confession, giving of money, returning to the pawnbroker's apartment) are immediately followed by steps toward isolation (illness, refusal to confess, gratuitous insults). Yet the truth must surface and, at some level, the obsession must become explicit. Thus after a horrendous cat and mouse interview with Porfiry

Petrovich, and after being accused of murder by a complete stranger, Raskolnikov, "with shaking knees and a feeling of frozen horror," reaches his lodging and collapses with disconnected sights and thoughts whirling through his head:

1   He lost consciousness; it seemed to him strange that he
        could not remember how he had come to be in the street.
        It was already late evening. Dark was coming on fast, the
        full moon was shining brighter and brighter; but there
5   was something particularly stifling about the air. People
        were walking in crowds along the streets; artisans and
        busy people were going home, others were out for a
        walk; there was a smell of whitewash, dust, stagnant
        water. Raskolnikov walked along sad and preoccupied:
10   he remembered very well having left the house with
        some kind of intention, that he had to do something and
        quickly, but what it was exactly, he had forgotten. Suddenly
        he stopped and saw that on the other side of the
        street, on the sidewalk, a man was standing and waving
15   at him with his hand. He crossed over the road to him,
        but suddenly this man turned on his heel and walked off
        as though nothing had happened, his head low, not turning
        round and not looking at him though he had summoned
        him. "Really now, did he call me?" Raskolnikov
20   wondered, but nevertheless began to catch up with him.
        He had not gone ten paces when suddenly he recognized
        him, and took fright: this was the man he had seen before,
        in the same smock and just as hunchbacked. Raskolnikov
        followed him at a distance; his heart was pounding;
25   they turned into a side street, but the man still did
        not look back. "Does he know that I am following him?"
        Raskolnikov wondered. The man entered the gate of a
        large house. Raskolnikov hurried up to these gates and
        began to look to see whether he would turn round and
30   summon him. Indeed, having passed through the gateway,

108

and already entering the courtyard, the man suddenly turned round and again seemingly waved to him in exactly the same way. Raskolnikov immediately went through the gateway, but now the man was no longer in the courtyard. He must therefore immediately have entered the first staircase. Raskolnikov rushed after him. Sure enough, two flights higher he could hear somebody's measured, unhurried footsteps. The staircase seemed strangely familiar! There was the window on the first floor with the moonlight coming through sadly and mysteriously; and here was the second floor. Hah! This was the same apartment in which the workmen had been painting. . . . Why hadn't he recognized it immediately? The steps of the man walking ahead died away: "He must have stopped or hidden somewhere." Here was the third floor; should he go on? And how quiet it was there, even frightening. . . . But he went on. The sound of his own footsteps frightened and disturbed him. God! How dark it was! The man must be hiding somewhere here in a corner. Ah! the apartment was wide open to the staircase; he thought a moment and went in. In the foyer everything was dark and empty, there was not a soul, as though everything had been taken away; softly, on tiptoe, he went through into the sitting room: the whole room was brightly lit by moonlight; everything was the same here: chairs, the mirror, the yellow divan and the pictures in frames. A huge, round copper red moon was looking right through the window. "This silence is because of the moon," Raskolnikov thought, "he must be setting a riddle now." He stood and waited, he waited a long time and the quieter the moon the harder his heart pounded; it was beginning to hurt. And there was still silence. Suddenly he heard a momentary dry snapping noise, as though someone had broken a splinter and everything was again dead still. A fly that had woken up suddenly flew against a window pane and began to buzz piteously. At this very moment in a corner, between a

small cupboard and the window, he could make out
what looked like a woman's dress hanging on the wall.
70 "Why is this dress here?" he thought. "It was not here
before. . . ." He went up softly and figured that someone
seemed to be hiding behind the dress. He carefully drew
aside the dress with his hand and saw that there was a
chair standing here, and on the chair in a corner was sit-
75 ting the little old woman, all hunched up and with bent
head, so that he could not make out her face; but it was
she. He stood over her a moment; "She is frightened!"
he thought, quietly took the axe from its noose, and
struck the old woman on the crown of the head, once
80 and then again. But strange to say she did not even
budge at these blows, as though she was made of wood.
He was frightened, bent down closer and began to examine her; but she bent her head down even further. He
then bent down right to the floor and looked into her
85 face from below—he looked and went numb: the old
woman was sitting there and laughing, she was simply
convulsed by silent, inaudible laughter, restraining herself as hard as she could so that he should not hear her.
Suddenly it seemed to him that the door from the bed-
90 room had opened slightly and that there too, there were
people laughing and whispering. He was overcome by
rage! With all his might he began to hit the old woman
on the head, but with each blow of his axe the laughter
and whispering from the bedroom became louder and
95 more audible, and the old woman was simply rocking
with laughter. He started to run, but the whole foyer
was already full of people, the doors and the staircase
were open wide, and on the landing, in the staircase and
down below, there were people, one after another, all
100 looking,—but they were all waiting with bated breath,
silently! . . . His heart missed a beat, his lips would not
move, they were rooted to the spot . . . he tried to shout
and—woke up.
　　He drew a deep breath, but the dream seemed

110

strangely to be continuing: his door was wide open and
on the threshold stood a complete stranger, looking fixedly at him. (Vol. V, pp. 286-288)

On a Matter of Capital Punishment

It becomes quickly apparent that Raskolnikov's
third dream is heavily colored by two scenes of the
novel—the actual murder of the pawnbroker and the
murderer's compulsive return to the scene of the crime.
The dream thus brings past-action back into the present
and catalyzes the hero's conscious and unconscious fears.

To investigate the possible sources of the dream
that may lie outside the chronology of the novel, we
now shall turn to one of Hugo's early works, *Le Dernier
Jour d'un condamné* (1829), and point out the resemblances between one passage of that work and the
above excerpt from *Crime and Punishment*.

Victor Hugo's reasons for writing *Le Dernier Jour
d'un condamné* are well known. Since in those days the
execution of criminals was carried on in public, he had
been the unwilling and horrified witness of a number of
guillotinements. Then there was one too many of these
chance encounters:

M. Victor Hugo revit la guillotine un jour qu'il traversait, vers
deux heures, la place de l'Hôtel de Ville. Le bourreau répétait la
représentation du soir; le couperet n'allait pas bien, il graissa les
rainures, et puis il essaya encore; cette fois il fut content. Cet
homme, qui s'apprêtait à en tuer un autre, qui faisait cela en plein
jour, en public, en causant avec les curieux, pendant qu'un mal-
heureux homme désespéré se débattait dans sa prison, fou de
rage, ou se laissait lier avec l'inertie et l'hébêtement de la terreur,
fut pour M. Victor Hugo une figure hideuse, et la répétition de la

chose lui parut aussi odieuse que la chose même.

Il se mit le lendemain même à écrire *Le Dernier Jour d'un condamné*, et l'acheva en trois semaines.[2]

If appeals are rejected, the death sentence of a criminal is to be carried out six weeks after the condemnation. During his last week Hugo's "condemned man" begins writing a desperate journal in which happy memories of the past and impossible fantasies of the future mingle, while he analyses minutely the horror of his position and the agony of fear and waiting he is experiencing. The act of writing is the unfortunate man's ultimate contact with the world of the living[3] and his only means of alleviating the sufferings that come from being "seul à seul avec une idée, une idée de crime et de châtiment, de meurtre et de mort!"

The condemned man is young, educated, rather well off, married, and the father of a three-year-old girl. However, the reader never learns the hero's name, nor the exact nature of his crime, although there is no doubt that he did commit one.[4] The story of his life is never put down on paper[5] and therefore throughout the novel the emphasis is on his anguish as a human being rather than as a specific individual.[6] Some two hours before his execution, the condemned man is overcome by his last mortal sleep:

1   J'ai fait un rêve.
            J'ai rêvé que c'était la nuit. Il me semblait que j'étais dans mon cabinet avec deux ou trois de mes amis, je ne sais plus lesquels.
5   Ma femme était couchée dans la chambre à coucher, à côté, et dormait avec son enfant.
            Nous parlions à voix basse, mes amis et moi, et ce que nous disions nous effrayait.

Tout à coup il me sembla entendre un bruit
10 quelque part dans les autres pièces de l'appartement: un
bruit faible, étrange, indéterminé.

Mes amis avaient entendu comme moi. Nous écou-
tâmes; c'était comme une serrure qu'on ouvre sourdement, comme un verrou qu'on scie à petit bruit.
15 Il y avait quelque chose qui nous glaçait: nous
avions peur. Nous pensâmes que peut-être c'étaient des
voleurs qui s'étaient introduits chez moi, à cette heure si
avancée de la nuit.

Nous résolûmes d'aller voir. Je me levai, je pris la
20 bougie. Mes amis me suivaient, un à un.

Nous traversâmes la chambre à coucher, à côté. Ma
femme dormait avec son enfant.

Puis nous arrivâmes dans le salon. Rien. Les portraits étaient immobiles dans leurs cadres d'or sur la ten-
25 ture rouge. Il me sembla que la porte du salon à la salle
à manger n'était point à sa place ordinaire.

Nous entrâmes dans la salle à manger; nous en
fîmes le tour. Je marchais le premier. La porte sur l'escalier était bien fermée, les fenêtres aussi. Arrivé près du
30 pôele, je vis que l'armoire au linge était ouverte, et que
la porte de cette armoire était tirée sur l'angle du mur,
comme pour le cacher.

Cela me surprit. Nous pensâmes qu'il y avait quel-
gu'un derrière la porte.
35 Je portai la main à cette porte pour refermer l'armoire; elle résista. Etonné, je tirai plus fort, elle céda
brusquement, et nous découvrîmes une petite vieille, les
mains pendantes, les yeux fermés, immobile, debout, et
comme collée dans l'angle du mur.
40 Cela avait quelque chose de hideux, et mes cheveux se dressent d'y penser.

Je demandai à la vieille:

—Que faites-vous là?

Elle ne répondit pas.
45 Je lui demandai:

113

—Qui êtes-vous?

Elle ne répondit pas, ne bougea pas, et resta les yeux fermés.

Mes amis dirent:

50 —C'est sans doute la complice de ceux qui sont entrés avec de mauvaises pensées; ils se sont échappés en nous entendant venir; elle n'aura pu fuir, et s'est cachée là.

Je l'ai interrogée de nouveau; elle est demeurée
55 sans voix, sans mouvement, sans regard.

Un de nous l'a poussée à terre, elle est tombée.

Elle est tombée tout d'une pièce, comme un morceau de bois, comme une chose morte.

Nous l'avons remuée du pied, puis deux de nous
60 l'ont relevée et de nouveau appuyée au mur. Elle n'a donné aucun signe de vie. On lui a crié dans l'oreille, elle est restée muette comme si elle était sourde.

Cependant, nous perdions patience, et il y avait de la colère dans notre terreur. Un de nous m'a dit:
65 —Mettez-lui la bougie sous le menton.

Je lui ai mis la mèche enflammée sous le menton. Alors elle a ouvert un oeil à demi, un oeil vide, terne, affreux, et qui ne regardait pas.

J'ai ôté la flamme et j'ai dit:
70 —Ah! enfin! répondras-tu, vieille sorcière? Qui es-tu?

L'oeil s'est refermé comme de lui-même.

—Pour le coup, c'est trop fort, ont dit les autres. Encore la bougie! encore! il faudra bien qu'elle parle.

J'ai replacé la lumière sous le menton de la vieille.
75 Alors, elle a ouvert ses deux yeux lentement, nous a regardés tous les uns après les autres, puis, se baissant brusquement, a soufflé la bougie avec un souffle glacé. Au même moment j'ai senti trois dents aiguës s'imprimer sur ma main dans les ténèbres.
80 Je me suis réveillé, frissonnant et baigné d'une sueur froide.

Le bon aumônier était assis au pied de mon lit, et

114

lisait des prières.[7]

It has by now become apparent that our "model dream" is a synopsis of both the Russian nightmare of Rodion Raskolnikov and the French nightmare of the condemned man. The parts of the two dreams that could not be reduced to a common denominator have been left out of the model, and the parallel details have been stressed. Nonetheless—despite our suppression of some differences between the two texts—the model dream is surprisingly faithful to both Hugo's and Dostoevsky's oneiric creations. How then do we explain the common features that will have caught any reader's eye?

Aspects of the Russian Literary Fate of Hugo's Condemned Man.

The basic theme of *Le Dernier Jour d'un condamné* reflects Hugo's early humanitarian concerns which will find their fullest expression in *Les Misérables*. The earlier work is, in the words of Jean-Bertrand Barrère, "un roman d'introspection, concentré sur l'évolution mentale d'un condamné";[8] it is also a passionate pamphlet against capital punishment, and it was to be looked upon by the Russian "progressive" intelligentsia as an outstanding example of humanitarian and social interest.[9] Since the book had rapidly become part of the Russian literary tradition, it is reasonable to assume that Dostoevsky was well aware of it. In fact, in this instance one can go beyond assumptions, for again the illuminating link is provided by Dostoevsky himself, in a letter of December 22, 1849, to his brother (Vol. I, pp. 128-31).

115

Dostoevsky writes of the reprieve granted by the Emperor, of the condemnation to hard labor and, above all, of the perfect joy of being alive. Alive, no matter where, a human being can "love, and suffer, and pity, and remember." Alive, "on voit le soleil!" This short exclamation in French, completely integrated into his text by Dostoevsky, has only recently been seen as worthy of exegesis.[10] Yet it reveals one of those instances where fiction and reality converge. What had happened to Dostoevsky and his companions on that fateful December 22nd was literally what Hugo's condemned man had so desperately wished for—the commutation of the death sentence for life imprisonment as a convict. Chapter XXIX of *Le Dernier Jour* is but one cry for such a miracle.

Oh! ma grâce! ma grâce! on me fera peut-être grâce. Le roi ne m'en veut pas. Qu'on aille chercher mon avocat! vite l'avocat! je veux bien des galères. Cinq ans de galères, et que tout soit dit,— ou vingt ans,—ou à perpétuité avec le fer rouge. Mais grâce de la vie!

Un forçat, cela marche encore, cela va et vient, *cela voit le soleil*. (Our italics)

The person here is stripped of all superfluities. What is left is the bare physical freedom of survival. A convict, albeit restricted by definition, can move his limbs (*marche* encore), occupy a given space *(va et vient)*, can experience light and warmth. The metaphorical association is obvious, for where there is sun there is organic life. The condemned man is reified by the law— the triple use of the neutral form of the demonstrative *cela* connotes lack of personal traits. The indefinite *on* as used by Dostoevsky conveys the same message,

116

somewhat humanized. Yet despite such reification, one still has a *head*, one is alive enough to see the sun. Thus besides being an attack on capital punishment, *Le Dernier Jour* graphically describes—one could almost say documents—the obsessional states associated with deprivation of freedom of choice, with its ensuing social isolation, psychological disintegration, and ontological terror. The images touch the very core of existence. We hardly need to ponder whether Dostoevsky had read *Le Dernier Jour d'un condamné* before or after 1838[11] or how many times he read it. What is worthy of scrutiny is that the first act of the "condemned" Fyodor—namely the writing of a letter to Mikhail—is to acknowledge that although he is alive, the old "head" has been "severed from his shoulders." He will therefore be different, but there should be a future for a surviving writer. What appears to be occurring is a movement from what had been Dostoevsky's exemplar intuitive understanding of Hugo's writing to a complete emotional identification with the content of that writing. Dostoevsky was not condemned to beheading but to the firing squad. Going beyond questions of literary remembrances, we can see reality acting here as a catalyst to literature.

It should be small wonder, then, if a number of the post-Siberian works, besides *Crime and Punishment*, show traces of a sustained attachment to the themes and semantics of Hugo's short masterpiece.

* * *

In Chapters I and V of *The Idiot* (1868) the reader gains much insight into Prince Myshkin's character as well as into Dostoevsky's own views on the death penalty. The Prince's two lengthy accounts[12] of an execution he witnessed while traveling in France bear a striking resemblance in tone and details to *Le Dernier Jour*.

It is done in an instant. The man is laid down, and a sort of broad knife falls down heavily, with tremendous force, on the machine—which is called a guillotine. In less than a second, the head is cut off. The preliminaries are awful. When they read out the death sentence, get the man ready for execution, tie him up, carry him up on the scaffold—all that is horrible! . . . What is going on with the soul at that moment, what convulsions does it suffer? It is an outrage on the soul and nothing else. . . . Yet the chief and worst pain is perhaps not inflicted by wounds, but by your certain knowledge that in an hour, in ten minutes, in half a minute, now, this moment, your soul will fly out of your body, and that you will be a human being no longer, and that that's certain—the main thing is that it is certain. . . (H)ere you have been sentenced to death, and the whole terrible agony lies in the fact that you will most certainly not escape, and there is no agony greater than that. (Vol. VI, pp. 25-26)

Note how in these lines Dostoevsky has collapsed several themes that appear scattered throughout Hugo's work.

Maintenant je suis captif. Mon corps est aux fers dans un cachot, mon esprit est en prison dans une idée. Une horrible, une sanglante, une implacable idée! Je n'ai plus qu'une pensée, qu'une conviction, qu'une certitude: condamné à mort. (I, 322) Eh! qu'est-ce donc que cette agonie de six semaines et ce râle de tout un jour? Qu'est-ce que les angoisses de cette journée irréparable, qui s'écoule si lentement et si vite? Qu'est-ce que cette échelle de tortures qui aboutit à l'échafaud? (XXXIX, 424) (M)oins qu'une minute, moins qu'une seconde, et la chose est faite. —Se sont-ils jamais mis, seulement en pensée, à la place de celui qui est là, au moment où le lourd tranchant qui tombe mord la chair, rompt les nerfs, brise les vertèbres. . . Mais quoi! une demi-seconde! la douleur est escamotée. . . . (XXXIX, 425) Il s'est mis à me lire un long texte. . . . —L'arrêt sera éxécuté aujourd'hui en place de Grève, a-t-il ajouté quant il a cu terminé, sans lever les yeux de dessus son papier timbré. Nous partons à sept heures et demie précises pour la Conciergerie. Mon cher monsieur, aurez-vous l'extrême bonté de me suivre? (XXI, 378-79) . . . tout à coup j'ai senti un froid d'acier dans mes cheveux, et les ciseaux ont grincé à mes oreilles. . . . Un jeune homme, . . . a demandé à un des guichetiers comment s'appelait ce qu'on faisait là. —La toilette du condamné, a répondu l'autre. (XLVIII, 444, 445)

When the Prince again tells the story to the Yepanchin girls, he describes not only what he actually saw and felt but also what he imagined the prisoner's last perceptions to have been. Myshkin's narrative reads very much like the descriptions—interspersed with identical specific details[13]—of the condemned man's final moments. Although Dostoevsky carried on where Hugo's narrator had to stop, that is, when the condemned man is about to be beheaded, the tone and tenor of his text remains very much in keeping with the frantic obsessiveness of the condemned man who can neither escape the fact that he is alive nor face the idea that he is dead.

And so it went on till he reached the plank. It is strange that one seldom faints during these very last seconds. On the contrary, the head is horribly alive and, I suppose, working hard, hard, hard like an engine going full speed. I imagine all sorts of thoughts—all unfinished, and absurd too, perhaps, and irrelevant, are throbbing to the last fraction of a second when his head already lies on the block and he waits, and he knows, suddenly he

119

hears the iron sliding down on his head (Vol. VI, p. 92)

As for *The Possessed* (1871), the late Soviet scholar V.V. Vinogradov devoted the larger section of his essay "From the Biography of a Certain 'Frenetic' Work" ("Iz biografii odnogo 'neistovogo' proizvedeniya")[14] to showing how material from *Le Dernier Jour* found its way into one of the key scenes of Dostoevsky's novel—the confrontation of Kirilov and Verkhovensky that precedes the former's suicide. In this instance, as in *Crime and Punishment*, elements from the condemned man's dream have been used. The mysterious role of the "old woman" is played by Kirilov, who, *silent and motionless, hides in the corner of a dark room between a wall and a cupboard. When the frightened and angry* Verkhovensky, who has a *candle*, finds Kirilov and stares at him, Kirilov remains stonelike but, suddenly, when the candle is brought close to his face, he knocks it away and savagely bites Verkhovensky's left hand.

Here Dostoevsky uses the candle, the burn, and the bite, which do not appear in *Crime and Punishment*. In *The Possessed*, however, these elements are incorporated into a real scene, not a dream, and the fearful and mysterious aspects are transferred from characters to the situation. In Vinogradov's words, "the nightmare of the condemned man, reworded in his own particular manner, is turned by Dostoevsky into a literary reality, into the actions of a suicide just before his death."[15]

These unacknowledged "borrowings" were followed by an arresting entry in Dostoevsky's publication *The Diary of a Writer* for November 1876. The entire installment is devoted to the short story *Krotkaya*, an internal monolog of "a husband whose wife is lying

120

before him on the table, having committed suicide a few hours previously by throwing herself out of the window." To meet the objection that such a story could not logically have been recorded on paper, Dostoevsky writes:

> But to some extent this sort of thing has been seen in literature before: Victor Hugo for example in his masterpiece *The Last Day of a Condemned Man* used almost the same device, and though he did not assume the presence of a stenographer, allowing himself an even greater improbability with the make-believe that a condemned man would have the opportunity (and the time) to make notes not only on his last day, but even at his last hours, and literally, at his last minute. But if he had not allowed himself this fantasy then the work itself would not exist—a work that is at once the most real and truthful of anything he wrote.[16]

It is clear that by 1876 *Le Dernier Jour* had long been assimilated into Dostoevsky's own creative system of reality and truth.

It is to Vinogradov's credit that he establishes a connection between *Le Dernier Jour* and a particular scene of *Crime and Punishment*: "In Dostoevsky's novel where the image of the old woman, who is killed by Raskolnikov and destroys him, appeared as the symbol of a complex structure and sharp semantic focus, there are obvious fragments of Hugo's symbolism, though they have been subjected to a peculiar 're-interpretation.' "[17] But Vinogradov indicates neither how such a "re-interpretation" was achieved nor the workings of "Hugo's symbolism" in the Dostoevskian context.

Certainly Raskolnikov's third dream resembles Hugo's text, and its sequence of events parallels in part the condemned man. Vinogradov points out some

121

similarities that could not have been accidental:

In the composition of [Raskolnikov's] dream it is easy to see the structural elements which it shares with the dream of [Hugo's] "condemned man"—search of the rooms, the appearance of the living room, the place in the corner behind the cupboard where the old woman hid, the old woman's wooden immobility, the [criminal's] scrutiny of her, the way he tortures her.[18]

Although the above listing is quite accurate, its incompleteness invites a new examination of the two texts. In the table that follows, the quotations are followed by numbers in parentheses corresponding to the line numberings of the original excerpts quoted above. This should draw attention to any differences or changes in sequence of the two authors' original order or, even more, in this case, to the paucity of such differences or changes. Some of the more elusive (and in some cases debatable) points of contact between the two lists are italicized.

Crime and Punishment	*Le Dernier Jour d'un condamné*
1. He lost consciousness. . . . (1)	1. J'ai fait un rêve. (1)
2. It was already late evening. (3)	2. J'ai rêvé que c'était la nuit. (2)
3. Sure enough, two flights higher up, he could hear somebody's measured, unhurried footsteps. (37-8)	3. Tout à coup il me sembla entendre un bruit quelque part dans les autres pièces de l'appartement; . . . (10)
4. The staircase seemed strangely *familiar*. . . . This was the *same* apartment. . . . (38-9)	4. Il me semblait que j'étais dans *mon* cabinet. . . . *Ma femme*. . . . (2-3, 5)
5. . . . moonlight . . . here was	5. . . . je pris la bougie. . . .

122

the second floor. . . . (40-1)

6. The steps of the man walking ahead died away. . . . Here was the third floor. . . . (44, 45-6)

7. And how quiet it was up there, even frightening. (46-7)

8. The sound of *his own* footsteps frightened and disturbed him. (47-8)

9. The man *must be* hiding *some*where here in a corner. (49-50)

10. . . . the apartment was wide open . . . he . . . went in.
In the foyer everything was dark and empty, there was not a soul. . . . (50-3)

11. . . . he went . . . into the sitting room. . . . (54)

12. . . . everything was *the same* here: chairs, the mirror, *the y*ellow divan, and the pictures in the *frames.* (55-7)

13. "This silence is because of the moon. . . ." (58-9)

14. Suddenly he heard a momentary dry snapping noise. . . A *fly* . . . began to buzz piteously. (65-7)

15. . . . in the corner, between a small cupboard and the window, he could make out what

Nous traversâmes la chambre à coucher. . . . (19, 21)

6. Puis nous arrivâmes dans le salon. Rien. (23)

7. Il y avait quelque chose qui nous glaçait ; nous avions peur. (15-16)

8. . . . et ce que *nous* disions nous effrayait. (7-8)

9. Nous pensâmes que peut-être c'étaient des voleurs. . . . (16-7)

10. Nous entrâmes dans la salle à manger ; . . . La porte sur l'escalier était bien fermée, les fenêtres aussi. (27-9)

11. (part of No. 6) . . . le salon. (23)

12. Les portraits étaient *immobiles* dans leurs *cadres d'or sur* la tenture rouge. (23-5)

13. (part of No. 12) . . . immobiles. . . . (24)

14. Tout à coup il me sembla entendre un bruit . . . c'était comme une serrure qu'on ouvre sourdement, comme un verrou qu'on scie à petit bruit. (13-14)

15. . . . je vis que l'armoire au linge était ouverte, et que la porte de cette armoire était tirée

123

looked like a woman's dress hanging on the wall. (67-9)

16. . . . in the corner, between a small cupboard and the window . . . [he] figured that someone seemed to be hiding behind the dress. (71-2)

17. He carefully drew aside the dress with his hand. . . . (72-3)

18. . . . [he] saw that there was a chair standing here, and and on the chair in a corner was sitting the little old woman, all hunched up . . . with bent head so that he could not make out her face. . . . (73-6)

19. "She is *frightened!*" he thought, . . . (77-8)

20. . . . took the ax from its noose and struck the old woman on the crown of the head, once and then again . . . she did not even budge at these blows, as though she were made of wood. (78-81)

21. . . . but she bent her head down even further (83)

22. He was frightened, . . . (82)

sur l'angle du mur, comme pour le cacher. (30-2)

16. Nous pensâmes qu'il y avait quelqu'un derrière la porte. (33-4)

17. Je portai la main à cette porte. . . . (35)

18. . . . nous découvrîmes une petite vieille, les mains pendantes, les yeux fermés, immobile, debout, et comme collée dans l'angle du mur. (37-9)

19. Cela avait quelque chose de hideux, et mes *cheveux se dressent* d'y penser. (40-1)

20. Je demandai à la vieille:
—Que faites-vous là?
     also:
. . . Je lui demandai:
—Qui êtes-vous? Elle ne répondit pas.
     also:
. . . elle est demeurée sans voix sans mouvement, sans regard.
. . . comme un morceau de bois
. . . . (54-5, 57-8)

21. . . . elle est tombée. . . . Elle est tombée tout d'une pièce.
. . . comme une chose morte. (56-8)

22. . . . et il y avait de la colère dans notre terreur. (63-4)

124

23. . . . the old woman was sitting there and laughing, she was simply convulsed by inaudible laughter, restraining herself as hard as she could so that he should not hear her. (85-88)

23. . . . ellc a ouvert un oeil à demi. . . . L'oeil s'est refermé comme de lui-même.
. . . elle a ouvert ses deux yeux lentement . . . a soufflé la bougie avec un souffle glacé . . . j'ai senti trois dents aiguës s'imprimer sur ma main. . . . (67, 71, 75-9)

24. He was overcome by rage! With all his might he began to hit the old woman on the head, . . . (91-3)

24. (part of No. 22) . . . de la colère dans notre terreur... Je lui ai mis la mèche enflammée sous le menton. (63-4, 66)

25. He tried to shout, and . . . woke up. (102-3)

25. Je me suis réveillé, frissonnant et baigné d'une sueur froide. (80-1)

26. . . . on the threshold stood a complete stranger, looking fixedly at him. (106-7)

26. Le bon aumônier était assis au pied de mon lit, et lisait des prières. (82-3)

Though tedious, this numerical listing is necessary to disclose parallels. Indeed, the narratives' frameworks, the action's dramatic progression, the heightening of the nervous tension, the specific devices used to create an atmosphere, the suspense, the mental anguish climaxing in physical violence, all echo each other. Structural and descriptive details seem to unfold side by side: dream (1), night (2), first noise (3), familiarity of locus (4), faint light (5), beginning of search (5,6), fear (7,8), possible intruder (9), prolonged search (10, 11), paintings in frames (12), silence, motionlessness (13), sudden new noise (14), suspicious corner (15), old woman in corner (16, 17, 18), fear (19, 22), woman's nonresponsiveness (20), she begins to alter position (21), she reacts (23), man's attack (24), dreamer's awakening (25), the stranger (26). Sheer coincidence can hardly be invoked, yet obvious alternative conclusions are difficult to draw. Perhaps the explanation of these parallels lies not so much in their evident similarities but in their differences, which we will examine now.

Differences between the Two Dreams

In point number four, we note that to Raskolnikov the staircase "seemed familiar," whereas the condemned man recollects being apparently in his own apartment. The "staircase" on which we have seen Raskolnikov three times before—on his way to rehearse his crime, on his way to the actual murder, and when afterwards he compulsively returned to the apartment—therefore links the dream with a crucial scene of the novel. This scene, in turn, triggers all further action and leads to the particular predicament in which Raskolnikov finds himself at the time of his dream. On the other hand, the condemned man's lodgings are a place of no further relevance to his somber tale.

In point number eight, although both men are scared of themselves, the specific sources of fear differ in the two texts. Raskolnikov's "own footsteps frightened and disturbed him." His fear comes from being alone in a place that has alarming connotations. On the other hand, the condemned man and his friends experience a fear that is connected to their conversation.[19] *(à voix basse)* late at night, but is not related to their surroundings.

Point number nine also brings out several discrepancies. "The man" whom Raskolnikov is following is a stranger whom he had met on the street and who had accused him of being a "murderer." The fear connected with past real events is carried into the dream and accounts for the definiteness of the threat—"The man must be hiding somewhere here in a corner." In the Hugo text, fear generates speculation *(nous pensâmes)* that certain persons *(des voleurs)* had broken into the house. But except for this notion—which would explain the purpose of the intruders—we have no specific knowledge of their presence or their location.

In point number twelve, Raskolnikov perceives the continuity between dream and reality by identifying particular pieces of furniture and "pictures in frames," whereas in the condemned man's dream the portraits that were "immobiles dans leurs cadres d'or" are used to convey both the lack of human presence and the silence. Dostoevsky communicates the awfulness of silence by reference to the moon and does not employ the picture device for that effect.[20] It is important though, that both authors use a kind of "dream-logic" to account for the silence. The causal factor varies in the two dreamers but the lack of a waking person's rationality is apparent to both.

In point number fourteen there is a sudden noise. The noise heard by the condemned man and his friends occurs early in this dream, and it stimulates a search of the apartment. But Raskolnikov hears a snapping noise after he has already gone through the premises—moreover, there is no equivalent in Hugo to Dostoevsky's use of "buzzing fly" as a double-edged image of symbol and reality. This fly, which interrupts the silence of Raskolnikov's dream, turns out to be in his room when he awakens. This fly is also, in a sense, related to Raskolnikov himself, imprisoned by seemingly invisible barriers.

Like an overlay in a film, a linking image is carried from one scene or sequence into the next. The detail thus sets off both the interlocking of dream and actual plot as well as the trapped state in which Raskolnikov finds himself, in dream and in real life. Such a device was neither needed nor employed in Hugo's story.

Several discrepancies should be noted in point number nineteen. First, it is the "little old woman" who is supposed to be frightened in Dostoevsky's text; but in Hugo's it is the dreamer who indicates his fear. Second, the degree of fear varies, as we can see by opposing "she is frightened" to "mes cheveux se dressent," which expresses terror rather than mere fright. The intensity of this emotion is underlined by the fact that the dreamer is terrified even in his recollection of that "hideous" moment of the dream. In contrast, we know nothing of the degree or the quality of fear imputed by Raskolnikov to Alena Ivanovna.

From this textual examination it would appear that the departures from Hugo's model (in which the connection between dream and reality is not made explicit), are all consistent with Raskolnikov's character and his actual experiences. In every point we have discussed, shifts have been made in keeping with the novel's thematic progression and it's hero's psyche. Place and motivation receive close attention in Dostoevsky's version. The critical point is reached when Dostoevsky introduces motivation into what was, in Hugo's original, an unmotivated scene. Hugo's "old woman" is very strange indeed, but we know nothing of her purposes; she eventually behaves in what might appear as a natural reaction to her tormentors: she fights back. In Raskolnikov's dreams, in contrast, motivation is introduced at the outset of his encounter with the old woman: Raskolnikov

128

attributes to her a fear that, in its very undoing, dramatizes his psychological weakness and his ambivalence. Dostoevsky's skill shows clearly in his ability to transform details of Hugo's text into indispensable aspects of character and plot.

Both our dreamers have very similar encounters and there is fear, anger, and physical violence in each case. But the content and thematic function of these meetings are very different. Hugo's dreamer is in his own apartment which he knows well, even in the dark. His wife and child are sleeping in another room and he is among friends. Frightened by an undetermined noise, they search the premises and find the old woman; but it is the way she looks more than her presence that is unnerving. As her questioners become angry, she blows out the candle and bites the dreamer instead of being attacked by him. Her behavior is frightening because of its context and unexpectedness, rather than because of its own violence. Even bitten, the man logically would be stronger than the old woman.

What we have here, and what gives the scene its impact, is not the senile aggressiveness of a hag, but the premonition of something cold *(souffle glacé)*, armed with teeth, which in darkness *(dans les ténèbres)* cuts the flesh. This is a rather apt description of the guillotine, which one readily can imagine as "immobile," "debout," "comme un morceau de bois," "comme une chose morte," until the lights go out and it bites. The stress all along is on physical danger that can attack at any time (even at night), and place (even in one's own home among friends), from any quarter (behind the cupboard), in any shape (an old lady). Furthermore, what the condemned man is fighting is the ominous presence of the monster so aptly called "la veuve" in

129

the slang of the prisons. This sinister widow will indeed cut him off forever from his dwelling, his friends, his wife and child, from everything that makes him a member of society. As the chosen instrument of "Justice," it will sever his head and he will be eliminated, physically, socially, and legally. It is well worth noticing that when Hugo's dreamer awakens he sees at his bedside the familiar figure of a priest—the link between both the afterworld to which he is bound and the established order that commands his death.

Things are not quite the same for Raskolnikov. To begin with, he is not in his apartment but is led to "a large house." He climbs four flights of stairs before entering *the* apartment, and only on the second floor does he begin to "recognize" the place. His knowledge of the locale is in no way reassuring but, on the contrary, he finds the situation strange and disturbing. Moreover, a particular twist is given to the "quietness," "the darkness," and the "familiarity" of the place by the fact that Raskolnikov is apprehending it all while going up a *staircase*—a *locus classicus* in itself for the dangers of the unknown and the metaphors of ascension and fall.[21]

Raskolnikov, having entered the third floor apartment, finds *his* "little old woman," whom he immediately recognizes. At this point a curious displacement of emotion occurs, for instead of being frightened himself, he assumes that "*she* is frightened"—of him.

This, of course, is quite different from what the condemned man experienced. Why then did Dostoevsky reverse something in his sources as central as the emotions of the main actors of the dream? It might be argued that, having been killed once by Raskolnikov, the old woman had ample cause for alarm and also that her fear was merely the projection of Raskolnikov's emotion in the face of his own crime. It might also be argued that the old woman's fear itself generates the ensuing assault, as if to justify her terror. Such a reversal of causes would establish a tension in the reader's mind that would last until released by the discovery that Raskolnikov's efforts are not only in vain, but are ludicrous. The frail old woman is rocking with silent laughter, not even acknowledging his person enough to laugh in his face. It is private, silent derision, an ultimate non-recognition in the face of his ultimate assertion of self. The more he hits her "with all his might," the more she laughs and by this means forces his retreat. At this point it becomes clear that for Raskolnikov to experience such a humiliation, the structure of the novel—in which the earlier encounters with the old woman had played such a decisive role—demanded that the emotions be transferred. Unlike the condemned man's agression, which triggered a response, Raskolnikov's show of strength is abysmally useless. Indeed, he is so powerless as to be laughable and, although unharmed, confronts much worse than physical danger or defeat, for he is threatened by the ultimate mortification—the loss of his identity. The old woman's laughter signifies that he has become a negligible entity, deprived even of the impact of his actions. The peril he faces is, therefore, ontological: the very meaning of his existence is at stake.

This danger of the unknown is not relieved when Raskolnikov awakes. In fact, he believes he is still dreaming, for what he sees is "a complete stranger looking fixedly at him." When the stranger introduces himself as Svidrigailov, the man who has harmed Raskolnikov's sister and mother, our dreamer is reminded that waking will not dispel the complications of his life.

Examined in this light, the two dreams, so similar

131

at the outset in their settings, suspenseful devices, and dramatic sequences, now appear to carry different meanings and to play different functions in their respective contexts. Paradoxically, the outward similarities in the description, pacing, and action of the two texts hide underlying dissimilarities in tone, structure and purpose. This apparent contradiction leads us to the question of why Dostoevsky needed Hugo's material in the first place and of how, given the differences, he could possibly have used it?

In order to suggest an answer we will reexamine our texts at their symbolic level. We noted that in *Le Dernier Jour d'un condamné*, the old woman who bites the dreamer can be understood as a projection and a premonition of the guillotine. As is well known, any condemned convict has to climb a flight of steps in order to reach the scaffold on which the machine stands. The condemned man, since he is writing his own story, cannot possibly describe these very last moments. But although the actual death scene is left for us to visualize, we feel that it is very much part of *Le Dernier Jour*, for the wretched narrator "lives" his death many times before his execution. During his last six weeks he imagines and suffers all the details of his agony to the extent of speculating about what he will feel at the precise instant the blade cuts into his neck.

Just as the monstrous machine looms throughout the story, the necessity of an ultimate climb is also very present. During his ordeal the condemned man goes up and down staircases and ladders to enter the courtrooms where he hears his condemnation, in and out of carts that carry him from one jail to another, and finally to the scaffold itself. At this point:

... la charrette s'est arrêtée subitement, et j'ai failli tomber la face sur les planches. Le prêtre m'a soutenu. —Courage! a-t-il murmuré. —Alors on a apporté une échelle à l'arrière de la charrette; il m'a donné le bras, *je suis descendu*, puis j'ai fait un pas, puis je me suis retourné pour en faire un autre, et je n'ai pu. Entre les deux lanternes du quai j'avais vu une chose sinistre.

oh! c'était la réalité!

Je me suis arrêté, comme chancelant déjà du coup.

—J'ai une dernière déclaration à faire! ai-je crié faiblement.

On m'a monté ici. (XLVIII, p. 454) (Our italics)

It could be argued here that the narrative required an incident that would delay the execution, so that the condemned man could actually write of his coming face to face with the guillotine. This need, however, could have been met without another climb, which can be interpreted as a last-minute rehearsal of the final one. Indeed, his supplications for grace being to no avail, the condemned man has to write his last sentence, "Ah! les misérables! Il me semble qu'*on monte* l'escalier. . . ." (our italics)

In such a context the last word—*escalier*—evokes most graphically the final climbing to his death. This brings us back to Raskolnikov ascending the "familiar" staircase on top of which he *knows* that death awaits, in the shape of an old woman who happens to have been an "official's widow."

This image of the staircase may serve to illustrate one way in which literary influence works. It shows how, by the grafting of a single detail onto Hugo's base, Dostoevsky was able to translate alien material into his own idiom, manipulating it, altering the atmosphere, shifting the emphasis, and transforming it to his own purpose and to reflect his own vision. In the beginning

133

the first text serves only as a seed. But later, in a process of total assimilation, it issues forth in a new organic literary creation.

Scrutinized in comparison with the condemned man's dream, Raskolnikov's third dream illustrates this process. It reveals two levels of similarities—the rather obvious one of character and action, and another more subtle similarity on the symbolic level. The dream of the condemned man, which has no prior reality in his life, functions only as a prefiguration of a future he has no power to alter. But Dostoevsky goes beyond this symbolization, for Raskolnikov's dream is a re-creation and transformation of past events and emotions in terms of dream logic. What forces itself on the dreamer will shape his waking hours. Through his dream he reformulates his view of his past and of himself, thus heightening dramatic tension and pushing the story towards its conclusion. The proximity and terror of death has become part of Raskolnikov's combat with himself. The outcome is still uncertain. The sequence of events is therefore altered to suit the psychological development of *Crime and Punishment.*

There remain, however, still other elements of Dostoevsky's text that cannot be explained in terms of any similarity (or dissimilarity) to Hugo's text. For example, there is no counterpart in the condemned man's dream to either the beginning or the end of Raskolnikov's dream. Our parallel begins only when Raskolnikov enters the house, not while he is walking in the streets or meeting a stranger. A whole passage is therefore omitted between points two and three in our table of parallels. The end of the dream, between points twenty-three and twenty-four, also had to be excerpted, leaving out the gathering of the crowd which laughs at Raskolnikov and prevents his escape. In order to investigate these differences, it may be useful to go back once more to our basic Hugo text, *Les Misérables*.

Jean Valjean, the Condemned Man, and Raskolnikov

En 1820, cinq ans après son arrivée à Montreuil-sur-mer, les services qu'il avait rendus au pays étaient si éclatants, le voeu de la contrée fut tellement unanime, que le roi le nomma de nouveau maire de la ville. (p. 170)

Ce fut la la troisième phase de son ascension. Le père Madeleine était devenu monsieur Madeleine, monsieur Madeleine devint monsieur le maire. (p. 171)

Monsieur Madeleine is, one has guessed, Jean Valjean who, thanks to his idea on how to modernize Montreuil's jewelry industry, had become the town's leading industrialist as well as the benefactor of the region.

On venait de dix lieues à la ronde consulter M. Madeleine. Il terminait les différends, il empêchait les procès, il réconciliait les ennemis. Chacun le prenait pour juge de son bon droit. Il semblait qu'il eût pour ame le livre de la loi naturelle. (p. 176)

This exemplary tale comes to an abrupt halt when the Mayor of Montreuil-sur-mer hears of the Champmathieu affair. This Champmathieu, an old vagabond, has been arrested for stealing some apples and taken to the departmental prison. There he was unhesitatingly recognized by an inmate as Jean Valjean, the ex-convict, an identity later confirmed by two other convicts as well as by Police Inspector Javert in person. The crux of the matter is that Valjean, although he served nineteen years in the galleys of Toulon, is not through serving time. Eight years before, he robbed a child of a silver coin—an offense that, compounded by the theft of an apple, is bound to send him back to the galleys for life.[22]

The case is to be tried on the day after Monsieur Madeleine hears of it, which does not leave him much time to decide whether he should expose himself, save a wretched old man, and destroy the venerable Mayor of Montreuil-sur-mer. Our hero's drama is acted out in one night and two celebrated chapters: "Une tempête sous un crane," in which Jean Valjean wrestles desperately with the alternative he faces, followed by "Formes que prend la souffrance pendant le sommeil." It is now in a sleeping man's subconscious—and through the special artistic technique of a dream—that the moral dilemma is apprehended.

Formes que prend la souffrance pendant le sommeil

Trois heures du matin venaient de sonner, et il y avait cinq heures qu'il marchait ainsi, presque sans interruption, lorsqu'il se laissa tomber sur sa chaise. Il s'y endormit et fit un rêve. Ce rêve, comme la plupart des rêves, ne se rapportait à la situation que par je ne sais quoi de funeste et de poignant, mais il lui fit impression. Ce cauchemar le frappa tellement que plus tard il l'a écrit. C'est un des papiers écrits de sa main qu'il a laissés. Nous croyons devoir transcrire ici cette chose textuellement.

Quel que soit ce rêve, l'histoire de cette nuit serait incomplète si nous l'omettions. C'est la sombre aventure d'une âme malade.

Le voici. Sur l'enveloppe nous trouvons cette ligne écrite: *Le rêve que j'ai eu cette nuit-là.*

"J'étais dans une campagne. Une grande campagne triste où il n'y avait pas d'herbe. Il ne me semblait pas qu'il fît jour ni qu'il fît nuit.

"Je me promenais avec mon frère, le frère de mes années d'enfance, ce frère auquel je dois dire que je ne pense jamais et dont je ne me souviens presque plus.

"Nous causions, et nous recontrions des passants. Nous parlions d'une voisine que nous avions eue autrefois, et qui, depuis qu'elle demeurait sur la rue, travaillait la fenêtre toujours ouverte. Tout en causant, nous avions froid à cause de cette fenêtre ouverte.

"Il n'y avait pas d'arbres dans la campagne.

"Nous vîmes un homme qui passa près de nous. C'était un homme tout nu, couleur de cendre, monté sur un cheval couleur de terre. L'homme n'avait pas de cheveux; on voyait son crâne et des veines sur son crâne. Il tenait à la main une baguette qui était souple comme un sarment de vigne et lourde comme du fer. Ce cavalier passa et ne nous dit rien.

"Mon frère me dit: Prenons par le chemin creux.

"Il y avait un chemin creux où l'on ne voyait pas une broussaille ni un brin de mousse. Tout était couleur de terre, même le ciel. Au bout de quelques pas, on ne me répondit plus quant je parlais. Je m'aperçus que mon frère n'était plus avec moi.

"J'entrai dans un village que je vis. Je songeai que ce devait être la Romainville (pourquoi Romainville?)

"La première rue où j'entrai était déserte. J'entrai dans une seconde rue. Derrière l'angle que faisaient les deux rues, il y avait un homme debout contre le mur. Je dis à cet homme: Quel est ce pays? où suis-je?

"L'homme ne répondit pas. Je vis la porte d'une maison ouverte, j'y entrai.

"La première chambre était déserte. J'entrai dans la seconde. Derrière la porte de cette chambre, il y avait un homme debout contre le mur. Je demandai à cet homme: —A qui est cette maison? où suis-je? L'homme ne répondit pas. La maison avait un jardin.

"Je sortis de la maison et j'entrai dans le jardin. Le jardin était désert. Derrière le premier arbre, je trouvai un homme qui se tenait debout. Je dis à cet homme: Quel est ce jardin? où suis-je? L'homme ne répondit pas.

"J'errai dans le village, et je m'aperçus que c'était une ville. Toutes les rues étaient désertes, toutes les portes étaient ouvertes. Aucun être vivant ne passait dans les rues, ne marchait dans les chambres ou ne se promenait dans les jardins. Mais il y avait derrière chaque angle de mur, derrière chaque porte, derrière chaque arbre, un homme debout qui se taisait. On n'en voyait jamais qu'un à la fois. Ces hommes me regardaient passer.

"Je sortis de la ville et je me mis à marcher dans les champs.

"Au bout de quelque temps, je me retournai, et je vis une grande foule qui venait derrière moi. Je reconnus tous les hommes que j'avais vus dans la ville. Ils avaient des têtes étranges. Ils ne semblaient pas se hâter, et cependant ils marchaient plus vite que moi. Ils ne faisaient aucun bruit en marchant. En un instant, cette foule me rejoignit et m'entoura. Les visages de ces hommes étaient couleur de terre.

"Alors le premier que j'avais vu et questionné en entrant dans la ville me dit: —Où allez-vous? Est-ce que vous ne savez pas que vous êtes mort depuis longtemps?

"J'ouvris la bouche pour répondre, et je m'aperçus qu'il n'y avait personne autour de moi."

Il se réveilla. Il était glacé. (pp. 247-49)

The three dreams under study clearly comply with the basic tenets of literary realism. In each case the author establishes a clear delineation between waking and sleeping states. The hero has fallen asleep, is actually dreaming and, in the end wakes up. The dream, although an integral part of the unconscious flow, has a stylistic and semantic unity of its own. The dream is linked to reality, however, through a concrete detail. There is an actual fly in Raskolnikov's room. The dreaming Valjean is very cold because the window of the actual room has remained open. Rules of verisimilitude are also respected inasmuch as Jean Valjean is said to have written his own dream. In the whole of *Les Misérables* this is the only such dream.[23] It is also an instance of a narrative written in the first person, thus coming close to the more contemporary interior monolog. The fact that Valjean's voice can be heard without an intermediary has multiple implications.[24] We see a man who has managed to survive thanks to his chameleonic skill at assuming new identities, whose life has been spent in hiding, who has had to suppress emotions and traits that might give him away. In the dream, at the moment when Mr. Madeleine could make Jean Valjean disappear (just as surely as the long-lost brother vanishes), the *"je"* is forced to the surface and confronted with great perils. Supposing that Champmathieu could be made to assume Valjean's social identity, would Valjean be replaced in body only? By abandoning a brother (Champmathieu, his other self?) could he gain his rightful place in the sun? Or would he be betraying a brotherhood of a higher order? Can resurrection be compartmentalized?

In view of such questions we should not be too surprised that Jean Valjean's dream intersects Raskolnikov's third dream at several points. The first discernible parallels take us back to the first part of the Russian character's dream. Both Valjean and Raskolnikov walk aimlessly at twilight through the streets of a city. Although Valjean is supposed to be in the country, all the details are given negatively to describe a nonrural setting: ". . . il n'y avait pas d'herbe . . . pas d'arbres. . . . J'errai dans le village, et je m'aperçus que c'était une ville." In both dreams the streets are crowded. One passerby is singled out for his extraordinary appearance or behavior. This stranger leads the dreamer to a house with a courtyard or garden, and he enters. Both guides remain silent, then disappear. In Valjean's case the world is populous but impersonal, filled with shadowy strangers. Valjean leaves the house. Raskolnikov remains, and at this juncture his dream adopts the pattern of the condemned man's dream.

Another important parallel appears at the end of both dreams. All exits are then blocked by a crowd of silent ghosts. The dreamers are trapped. Jean Valjean had resumed his wandering:

Ils avaient des têtes étranges. Ils ne semblaient pas se hâter, et cependant ils marchaient plus vite que moi. Ils ne faisaient aucun bruit en marchant. En un instant, cette foule me rejoignit et m'entoura.

As for Raskolnikov:

He started to run, but the whole foyer was already full of people, the doors and the staircase were open wide, and on the landing, in the staircase and down below, there were people, one after another, all looking —but they were all waiting with bated breath, silently!

Petrified, unable to scream, he wakes up. Although Valjean is, at least, addressed by a member of the crowd, the questions asked are so rhetorical that no one remains to hear the answers. Action itself will reply when Jean Valjean denounces himself.

* * *

In sum, the two Hugo dreams together provide most of the narrative material used and transformed in the composition of Raskolnikov's third dream. Jean Valjean, the condemned man, and Raskolnikov are all overcome by exhaustion, each gives in to sleep but not to

140

forgetfulness. Reality becomes nightmare that in turn mirrors the *idée fixe*, the fears and anxieties of the dreamers. The dream of the condemned man is not causally linked to the progression of the action; it has no bearing on his case. Though unrelated to objective reality, however, his dream reflects subjective reality. The danger in the dream is symbolic of the very real danger threatening him in life. While the dream does not alter the course of the drama, it functions as a psychological device to heighten the pathetic aspects of the hero's predicament.

Unlike the condemned man's, Valjean's dream functions as an integral part of the plot. It not only is stimulated by mental torments inherent in the situation, but it also stimulates further action, since it gives the dreamer the answer he sought while awake. The climax of the dream and the clue to decoding its meaning are found in the question one of the ghosts asks: "Où allez-vous? Est-ce que vous ne savez pas que vous êtes mort depuis longtemps?" From his dream Jean Valjean learns what will happen to him if he lets another human being bear his own burden. Although seemingly he would remain physically well, he would betray God, sever his bond with nature, and compromise irrevocably his striving toward salvation. As in his dream—which is of course a descent to Hades—he would become a soulless body—cut off from the world like those who have crossed the Styx. But even as a convict in chains he can save his soul without sacrificing the ideal of human fraternity. Having understood this through the intrument of his nightmare, Valjean must confess to being who he is.

The condemned man was, we gather, a basically honest man who fell into crime and now faces society's retribution. Jean Valjean was a basically honest man of whom, for a minor offense, society made a hardened criminal. Through repentance he comes to peaceful terms both with his conscience and with society which, in the persons of Javert and Marius, acknowledges his transformation. Like both of them, Raskolnikov is honest *and* criminal, and thus dreams a dream compounded from their two. Like the condemned man, he is unable to come to terms with social laws and so dreams of a murderous assault. Like Jean Valjean, he is struggling with elemental concepts of good and evil, and dreams of himself as trapped in a place as desolate and stifling as Jean Valjean's Hell.

What tortures Raskolnikov before he falls asleep is not only that he was able to commit murder, but even more that he is not able to accept himself as a murderer. "Perhaps the old woman was a mistake, but she is not the point. . . . I wanted to pass on the other side . . . but . . . I did not do that. . . . The only thing I knew how to do was kill! And it turns out that I was not even able to do that. . ."(Vol. V, p. 285). What kind of "superman" is he, if he cannot live with the image of himself as a killer of old ladies, if the whole world laughs at him, if even his victim laughs at him? Raskolnikov wrestles with his conscience, with a deeply rooted sense of original sin, with the cerebral concept of a fate he wanted to create for himself. His dream does not solve his problems but only compounds his anguish and fear at not having become what he willed to be.

CONCLUSION: REALITY, IMAGINATION, FICTION

> Je commençai alors à soupçonner que toute cette af-
> faire pourrait mal tourner pour moi; mais une rétractation
> qu'il m'etait impossible d'appuyer d'aucune preuve devait
> m'être plus dangereuse que le silence. . . . Toutes ces idées
> m'agitèrent si vivement, que j'en fis une maladie. . . .
>
> *Vidocq,* Mémoires

Research that yields too many findings may become an embarrassment. Have we stumbled onto an example not only of literary influence but also of borrowing so extensive that we might have a case of blatant pla-
giarism? Could we then say that the author of *Crime
and Punishment* was at most a skillful repackager of another man's work?

The abundance and range of Dostoevsky's sources
is almost endless. Robert Belknap, in his inquiry into
"The Origins of Alëša Karamazov," points out how Dostoevsky created fiction out of his most diverse experiences—his own life, his conscious or unconscious memories, his journalistic activities, and his reading. "In Dostoevsky's creative laboratory, literary matter is neither
created nor destroyed."[1] An economy was imposed
even on material that he had already used and that years
later he might use again in a different context.

Belknap illustrates this method as follows:

143

Drawing from "Mixail," from Dickens, Cervantes, Pushkin, the Bible, a series of trials reported in the newspapers, and his own observations, Dostoevskij assembled the materials for a positively good man, set them to interact, and described the result in *The Idiot*.[2]

The problem was not abandoned with this experiment, however, for Prince Myshkin, a few incarnations later, will lend many recognizable traits to Alyosha Karamazov.

Though Dostoevsky's method is unusually complex, he obviously is not the only writer to use both literary and real-life sources as a substratum for his own fiction. Victor Hugo's journal, for example, published posthumously in 1887 under the title *Choses vues*, recounts numerous incidents—people seen, places visited, and scenes actually witnessed—that had been lived before they were fictionalized. One well-known instance of this is to be found in a chapter dated 1841 and entitled "L'Origine de 'Fantine.' "

Hugo tells how, while waiting for a carriage on his way home from a dinner party, he witnessed the following:

Il faisait ainsi le planton, quand il vit un jeune homme ficelé, et cossu dans sa mise, se baisser, ramasser une grosse poignée de neige et la planter dans le dos d'une fille qui stationnait au coin du boulevard et qui etait en robe décolletée.

Cette fille jeta un cri perçant, tomba sur le fashionable, et le battit. Le jeune homme rendit les coups, la fille riposta, *la bataille* all crescendo, si fort et si loin que les sergents de ville accoururent.

Ils empoignèrent la fille et ne touchèrent pas l'homme.[3]

His interest aroused, Hugo follows the group to the police station where he testifies as to what he saw and agrees to sign a deposition. This sets the woman free and spares her from a six-month jail term for "disturbing the peace."[4]

All the details of this experience were to serve as basic material for the celebrated episode in *Les Misérables* in which Fantine is victimized in the street, fights back, is arrested, and finally is extracted from Javert's clutches by Monsieur Madeleine, Mayor of Montreuil-sur-Mer. *Choses vues* documents the fact that this suspenseful scene—which provides a very good motive for Javert's renewed and resentful interest in the man he suspects of being Jean Valjean—was actually built upon a real incident and the emotional impact it had had on Hugo.

It may be interesting now to compare this recollection, which served as a source for fiction for the French writer, to a very different recollection of Dostoevsky. The account below is part of a rather forgotten memoir on Dostoevsky entitled "A Year with a Famous Writer" ("God raboty s znamenitym pisatelem") that appeared in 1904.[5] The author, a copy editor for the weekly *The Citizen*, met Dostoevsky, the editor-in-chief, on February 20, 1872. During the summer of that year Dostoevsky's family was in the country while he remained in St. Petersburg to fulfill his editorial duties. Mrs. Pochinkovskaya, who often worked into the night with Dostoevsky, had many opportunities to listen to his inspired monologues:

So now just imagine, continued Fyodor Mikhailovich with growing inspiration, imagine that something like this had happened to you. I recently heard about this case. This spring—it was like now,

145

at dawn—three young law students were returning home from a commencement supper. They were not drunk, not at all! They were sober, and even carrying on an exalted conversation with each other and declaiming verse. Well, they were reciting from Schiller's "The Hymn to Joy and Freedom." They were uttering the most pure and sublime words, as befits youth with ideals in its soul. And then here on the Nevsky, somewhere nearby, near the Church of the Apparition, they ran into a woman, one of those who walk the streets at night because this is their trade, and one by which they keep alive. . . . And so these youths, in an exalted mood and with an ideal in their souls (a favorite expression of Fyodor Mikhailovich to which he gave various senses by means of tone of voice), felt extreme disgust for this woman, faded, powdered, and raddled, selling her body. They were suddenly aware of such disgust for her and of such extremely great purity on their own part, that they all three spat in her face. And all three of them were taken, because of this, to the police station, to the Justice of the Peace. I saw them there and heard them— they were still rosy-cheeked and had scarcely any mustaches. And there, in the chambers of the Justice of the Peace, refusing to pay the fine for disorderly conduct, eloquently, in accordance with all the rules of higher scholarship, defended their legal right to behave just as they had behaved in the heat of their noble indignation at this bedraggled, venal creature.

He fell silent as though trying to remember what had happened next. Then he bent over to me slightly and said, dropping out the words expressively in order to make me feel the whole of their strength: What kind of notions about "exalted ideals" could these people have had, if they were able to do something so vulgar and despicable! And then to go on to defend their legal rights on the basis of higher scholarship! And what if they had made a mistake! What if they had not met that woman, but if instead you had chanced to encounter them and if your face, drawn by work and lack of sleep, had appeared to them worn out by debauchery—and they would have spat in your face! . . . And do you know I would be pleased if such a thing should happen to you. What a speech I would write for your defense![6]

146

This extraordinary account takes us far from Hugo's search for objectivity and his precise formulation of that search. On the contrary, the listener is involved with such immediacy and urgency that factual accuracy becomes the least important feature of this tirade. The reader, however, has the opportunity to ponder several questions. The core of the story might well be real, as Dostoevsky asserts. The encounter, at night, of students with a prostitute, is in itself an almost banal occurrence. But was our novelist actually at the police station when the three youths were taken there (as he says at the end of the account), or did he only hear about the incident (which is what he says at the outset)? The question of why he might have been at the police station promptly recedes as we witness what is happening there, listening to the students' rhetoric and looking at their rosy faces. Who could care about inconsistencies of fact while engrossed in such a wonderfully dramatic episode? Are the students made to pay their fine for disorderly conduct, or do they convince the Justice of the Peace of their purity and idealism? Again, who cares? Hardly do we have the time to be goaded into asking what goes through people's minds while they are committing "vulgar and despicable" acts than the problem is shifted from them to us, and the questioning becomes even more urgent. What would we do if, while minding our own business, we were spat upon by people who disliked our appearance? How would we feel? How would we react? Such things do happen and whether they are common or not, the very idea of their happening is unsettling. Because of the shock and pain and humiliation, our reaction might not be the most logical or objective. We might do strange things, very interesting things indeed, in the beholding of a novelist who has the intuitive

147

powers to imaginatively recreate our mental processes and then write about them.[7]

One way or another, there probably was some real basis for Dostoevsky's outburst, but what we have here, it seems, is an interpretation of both a fact of which Dostoevsky had knowledge, as well as of a fiction that is strongly reminiscent of a story à la Fantine, with Dostoevsky rather than Hugo in the role of Monsieur Madeleine. But regardless of the exact allocation of sources and roles, Dostoevsky's outburst can be read as an encapsulated model of the mechanisms by which original facts are distorted, dramatic tensions set up, and inspiration unlocked. By such a logic one might deduce from Dostoevsky's words to his copy editor the quintessence of the workings of literary influence. When recalled (or borrowed), the original material is made to fit a new situation and is given new implications that put the writer and the reader in the center of a scene quite different from its original model. When written material is the source, such a transformation can plausibly be reconstructed in the following manner: the reading alerts Dostoevsky and heightens his awareness of a certain kind of experience. The experience is further transferred into an imaginary context ("I would be pleased if such a thing should happen to you!") and into a Russian setting ("The Nevsky . . . the Church of the Apparition") and given a Russian mood ("ideal . . . soul . . . Schiller"). From then on the boundaries between fact and fiction become indistinct and the recreated experience finds its way into a conversation, into a "speech for [somebody's] defense" (as so often happens in *The Diary of a Writer*), or into a novel. Osmosis has occurred between the source and the new inspiration, the former being integrated in a manner befitting the new creative purpose.[8]

Processes similar to the ones we have uncovered certainly could be shown to have been at work in Dostoevsky's other novels as well. For example, the notebooks for *The Idiot* and *The Possessed*, as well as for *The Brothers Karamazov*, show references to specific passages from *Les Misérables*.[9] Moreover, the need we encountered in our own analysis to refer to other works of Hugo indicates that research could be expanded beyond *Les Misérables* to include the relationship of Dostoevsky to all of Hugo's works. Undoubtedly such inquiries would open new vistas to which different methods of investigation might have to be applied.

Further scholarship, however, should not be aimed at nailing down more and more connections, gradually encompassing literary reality until, at some distant time, it has been encircled and conquered. Scholarship should rather proceed in the sense of progressive revelation, in which each theory, each perspective on the author's works, reveals another immanence in our world. At its best, literary scholarship, like literature itself, should not only make things clear, which is to discover reality. It should also make things real, which is to create reality. Literature and literary criticism give existence to what, for us, otherwise would not have existed as an object of experience. Texts are not wild beasts to be trapped and tamed, but free creatures who, if properly studied, can illuminate our own creative freedom.

In the present essay we have had a more limited purpose. We have sought only to reveal the mechanisms by which materials from *Les Misérables* were transformed and redistributed once they had been apprehended by a kindred genius. The difference in technique in the two novels is motivated by a difference in intent. Hugo wanted to elicit pity for his characters and indignation for their plights. But Dostoevsky, by exploring the recesses of a soul who can choose to be good, compels the reader to "imagine that something like this" might have happened to him. Pity *for* persons in an unfortunate situation gives way to identification *with* people faced with a moral imperative. Concurrence to a vision of how society could be more humane gives way to compliance with the dictates of human conscience. The social novel of public activism becomes the psychological novel of personal redemption. Hugo's work foreshadowed a century of social protest; Dostoevsky's prefigured the alienation of contemporary man. Both authors, each in his own way, are moral prophets of the modern age.

NOTES

Chapter I

1. Melchior de Vogüé, *Le Roman russe* (Paris: Plon, Nourrit et Cie, 1866), p. 203.
2. John Middleton Murry, *Fyodor Dostoevsky: A Critical Study* (1924; reprint ed., New York: Russell and Russell, 1966), p. 29. Mr. Murry goes even further to suggest that:

> Dostoevsky was not a novelist, and he cannot be judged as a novelist. His superhuman figures do not differ from each other in the degree of their humanity; they are absolutely different, and it is in them that the strangeness and fascination and the power of Dostoevsky rests. (p. 48)

3. John Cowper Powys, *Dostoievsky* (London: John Lane, The Bodley Head, 1946), p. 87.
4. Since the post-Stalin era, publication of Dostoevsky's work as well as criticism of it has been steadily increasing in the Soviet Union. This progress is meticulously described in Vladimir Seduro, *Dostoevski's Image in Russia Today* (Belmont, Mass.: Norland, 1975). Here, however, we are considering Dostoevsky's image in the West.
5. E.g., L.P. Grossman, "Balzak i Dostoyevski," in *Poetika Dostoyevskogo* (Moscow, 1925), or A.L. Bem, "Pushkin i Dostoyevski" and "Gogol i Dostoyevski," in *O Dostoyevskom*, ed. A.L. Bem, Vol. III (Prague: Petropolis, 1936).
6. E.g., Charles Passage, *Dostoevski the Adapter: A Study in Dostoevski's Use of The Tales of Hoffman* (Chapel Hill, NC: Univ. of North Carolina, 1954); Donald Fanger, *Dostoevsky and Romantic Realism: A Study of Dostoevsky in Relation to Balzac, Dickens, and Gogol* (Cambridge: Harvard Univ., 1965); Edmund K. Kosta, *Schiller in Russian Literature* (Philadelphia: Univ. of Pennsylvania, 1965); Jean Weisgerber, *Faulkner et Dostoievsky: Confluences et influences* (Paris: Presses Universitaires de France, 1968); N.M. Lary, *Dostoevsky and Dickens: A Study of Literary Influence* (London and Boston: Routledge and Kegan Paul, 1973); and Alex de Jonge, *Dostoevsky and the Age of Intensity* (London: Secker and Warburg, 1975).
7. F.M. Dostoyevski, *Pisma [Letters]*, ed. A.S. Dolinin (Moscow: Goslitizdat, 1928-1959), Vol. I, p. 467. Subsequent references to the Dolinin edition of Dostoevsky's correspondence will be indicated by the volume and page number in parentheses following the quotation. This edition comprises four volumes published respectively in 1928, 1930, 1934, and 1959.
8. If young Dostoevsky's boast to his brother is at all accurate, it is an impressive accomplishment. Hugo, though only thirty-six at this time, had already published numerous volumes of poetry, prose, and drama, to wit:

Han d'Islande, 1823; *Bug-Jargal*, 1826; *Odes et Ballades*, 1826; *Cromwell*, 1827; *Marion Delorme*, 1828; *Les Orientales*, 1829; *Hernani*, 1830; *Le Dernier Jour d'un condamné*, 1829; *Notre-Dame de Paris*, 1831; *Feuilles d'Automne*, 1831; *Le Roi s'amuse*, 1832; *Lucrèce Borgia*, 1833; *Marie Tudor*, 1833; *Claude Gueux*, 1834; *Les Chants du Crépuscule*, 1835; *Angelo*, 1835; *Les Voix Intérieures*, 1836; and *Ruy Blas*, 1838.

9. Désiré Nisard (1806-1888), an eminent literary critic of the time, was a champion of the classical tradition in art; Nisard had little sympathy or understanding for the exponents of the Romantic School; he considered their work "litterature facile." Nisard published some six articles about Hugo, from 1829 to 1836. Chronological evidence as well as Dostoevsky's comments make it likely that the Russian author had read Nisard's last article about Hugo, entitled "M. Victor Hugo en 1836," originally published in *La Revue de Paris* in 1836 and 1837. A few lines from Nisard's prose should explain Dostoevsky's angry outburst:

> L'histoire des ouvrages de M. Victor Hugo est l'histoire de livres éphémères, greffés sur des lieux communs du jour ou imités d'ouvrages analogues, où le mérite de l'invention n'appartient pas à M. Victor Hugo. . . . Il a quelquefois exploité les découvertes d'autrui; mais il n'a jamais rien découvert. . . . Quelques lecteurs désintéressés . . . préfèrent la prose de M. Victor Hugo à ses vers. Ce n'est pas que cette prose soit de meilleure qualité en soi que sa poésie . . . c'est parce que les imperfection de M. Victor Hugo y sont plus supportables. . . .

In his conclusion Nisard foresaw "la mort littéraire de M. Victor Hugo" as "imminente" and "inévitable." See Désiré Nisard, *Essais sur l'école romantique* (Paris: Calmann-Levy, 1889), pp. 260, 269, 275.

10. See, for example, K. Mochulski, *Dostoyevski: zhizn i tvorchestvo* (Paris: YMCA, 1947), chaps. vi and vii; Avrahm Yarmolinsky, *Dostoevsky: His Life and Art* (New York: Criterion, 1957), chaps. iv, v, vi, and vii; E. H. Carr, *Dostoevsky: 1821-1881* (1931; reprint ed., London: Allen and Unwin, 1963), chaps. ii, iii, and iv; and Joseph Frank, *Dostoevsky: The Seeds of Revolt, 1821-1849* (Princeton: Princeton Univ., 1976), for the pre-Siberian period.

11. Yarmolinsky, *op. cit.*, p. 37.

12. Carr, *op. cit.*, p. 23.

13. At the beginning of 1846 a group of Russian intellectuals led by Mikhail Butashevich-Petrashevsky, an official of the Ministry of Foreign Affairs, had made a habit of gathering every Friday night in his apartment. The participants, united by their dislike of Nicholas I's regime and their feeling that political changes were needed, chiefly discussed church reform, liberation of the serfs, freedom of the press, and French utopian socialism. Although these discussions were not translated into actions, the Tsar, alarmed by the French Revolution of 1848 and its repercussions in Central Europe, decided to put an end to all such "subversive" activities. This historical episode is documented in a number of testimonies published in the Soviet Union. E.g., T.I. Usakina, *The Petrashevsky Circle and the Socioliterary Movement of the 1840s [Petrashevtsy i literaturno-obshchestvennoe*

dvizheniye sorokovykh godov] (Saratov, 1965); V.R. Leykina-Svirskaya, *The Petrashevsky Circle [Petrashevtsy]* (Moscow, 1965); V.V. Zhdanov, *Poets of the Petrashevsky Circle [Poety-Petrashevtsy]* (Leningrad, 1966), and N.F. Belchikov, *Dostoevsky in the Petrashevsky Trial [Dostoyevski v protsesse Petrashevtsev]* (Moscow, 1936), second ed. 1971.

14. Carr, *op. cit.*, p. 37.

15. "Gyugo i Dostoyevski: literaturny obzor," *Slavia* [Prague], Vol. XV (1937-1938), pp. 73-86.

16. "Winter Notes on Summer Impressions" ["Zimniye zametki o letnikh vpechatleniyakh"], which he published in *Vremya* in March 1863, is a scathing critique of most of what Dostoevsky saw in the English and French capitals.

17. The two ten-volume editions of Hugo's novel had come out in a series published simultaneously in Brussels and Paris from the end of March till the end of June 1862. *Cf.* Maurice Allem's "Notice Bibliographique" to his edition of *Les Misérables* ("Bibliothèque de la Pléiade"; Paris: Gallimard, 1960), pp. xix-xxiii.

18. Nikolai Nikolaevich Strakhov (1828-1896), a man of letters whom Dostoevsky met in the early sixties, was *Vremya*'s co-editor and literary critic. Vladimir Seduro, in his *Dostoyevski in Russian Literary Criticism: 1846-1856* (New York: Columbia University, 1957), p. 777, states that: "Strakhov's 'Reminiscences of Dostoyevski,' in the book published under the title *Biography of F.M. Dostoyevski: Letters and Notes from his Notebook, 1883 [Biografiya, pisma, zametki iz zapisnoy knizhki F.M. Dostoyevskovo, St. Petersburg, 1883]* is the most valuable contribution to the prerevolutionary biographical literature on Dostoyevski." Large excerpts of Strakhov's text have been reprinted in *F.M. Dostoyevski in the Recollections of his Contemporaries [F.M. Dostoyevski v vospominaniyakh sovremennikov]*, ed. A.S. Dolinin (2 vols.; Moscow, 1964). Strakhov's words quoted here are from Vol. I, pp. 299-300.

19. By Robert Louis Jackson, for example, in his discussion of Dostoevsky's concept of beauty. *Dostoevsky's Quest for Form: A Study of His Philosophy of Art* (New Haven: Yale University Press, 1966), pp. 68-69.

20. This of course is a reference to the literary controversy sparked by the publication in December 1827 of Hugo's historical drama *Cromwell* and, more specifically, by the stand Hugo took in the "Preface" to his play. This "Preface," written after the play but published simultaneously with it, has been considered ever since as the first French manifesto against the conventional tenets and literary rules of classicism, which in Hugo's view led to an incomplete portrayal of human reality. Instead, he advocated a new mode of expression that would free itself from the rules, from *unités* of time, place, and action, and from the interdiction against mixing literary genres. In so doing, this new mode would acknowledge and depict all aspects of human nature—*le beau et le laid*:

[La muse moderne] sentira que tout dans la création n'est pas humainement *beau*, que le laid y existe à côté du beau, le difforme près du gracieux, le grotesque au revers du sublime, le mal avec le bien, l'ombre avec la lumière.

V. Hugo, *Cromwell*, in *Oeuvres complètes de Victor Hugo* (édition *Ne va-rieter*, Vol. I, Paris: Hetzel, Quantin, 1880-1889), p. 16.

21. *Vremya*, No. 9 (September, 1862), pp. 44-46. Neither the "Intro-duction from the Editorial Staff" nor the translation of *Notre-Dame de Paris* were signed. Leonid P. Grossman established Dostoevsky's authorship of this "Introduction" and included it in his edition of Dostoevsky's *Complete Works [Polnoye sobraniye sochineni F.M. Dostoyevskogo]* (izd. "Prosveshcheniye"; Petrograd, 1911-1918), Vol. XXII, pp. 229-232. It subsequently was included in the 1930 edition of *Dostoevsky's Complete Works [Polnoye sobraniye khudozhestvennykh proizvedeni]*, ed. V. Toma-shevski and K. Khalabayev (Moscow-Leningrad, 1926-1930), Vol. XIII, pp. 525-527.

Grossman also attributes the translation of *Notre-Dame de Paris* to Dostoevsky, but the editors of the thirteen-volume edition of Dostoevsky's *Complete Works* considered it unlikely and attribute it to P. Smirnov (see *ibid.*, note on p. 607).

Except for *Eugénie Grandet*, which Dostoevsky translated in 1843, thus making his very first contribution to the world of letters, no full-length translations of his are known. It seems improbable that he could have translated *Notre-Dame de Paris* during the first half of 1862, if only for lack of time. On the other hand, both the style and content of the "Intro-duction" clearly bear his mark.

22. Hugo's and Dostoevsky's commonality of interests in social and ideological themes has prompted the following comment by G.M. Frid-lender in his "Les Notes de Dostoievsky sur Victor Hugo," pp. 288-294, in *Dostoievsky, L'Herne*, numéro 24 (Paris: Editions de l'Herne, 1973):

La préface de *Notre-Dame de Paris* n'a pas seulement été conçue par Dostoievski comme une interprétation du sens des romans de Hugo et comme leur appréciation artistique: elle a été aussi, en même temps, une *déclaration esthétique de Dostoievski lui-même*. (p. 292) [Frid-lender's italics]

As the first contribution on the Hugo-Dostoevsky literary relationship to come out of the Soviet Union in almost forty years, Fridlender's article is disappointing. It refrains from new elaboration or interpretation of known factual material and does little beside pointing toward a neglected field of investigation.

23. A.P. Milyukov (1817-1897), writer and literary historian, had been acquainted with Dostoevsky since the days of the Petrashevsky circle. His "Reminiscences of F. Dostoyevski" ["Vospominaniya o F. Dostoyev-skom"], were published in St. Petersburg in 1890. See *F.M. Dostoyevski v vospominaniyakh sovremennikov*, pp. 170-200.

24. See Edward Wasiolek's "Introduction" to his edition of F. M. Dos-toevsky, *The Notebooks for Crime and Punishment* (Chicago: University of Chicago Press, 1967), p. 4. The succession of catastrophes which befell Dostoevsky between 1863 and 1865—the forced suspension of *Vremya* by government censorship and the financial difficulties with his new journal *The Epoch [Epokha]*, his bondage to creditors, his recurrent epileptic fits,

the deaths of his first wife and of his brother Mikhail—amply explain his reduced output during these years. *Notes from the Underground [Zapiski iz
podpolya]* appeared in 1864.

25. Carr, *op. cit.*, p. 113.

26. *Dnevnik A.G. Dostoyevskoy: 1867 goda* (Moscow, 1923), p. 100.
In her *Memoirs*, written nearly fifty years later and which sometimes lack
the precision of her *Diary*, Anna Grigorevna remembers that in Geneva,
during the winter of 1867-68, Dostoevsky reread all of Balzac and George
Sand as well as "Victor Hugo's famous novel *Les humiliés et les offensés*"
(sic). *Vospominaniya A.G. Dostoyevskoy,* ed. L.P. Grossman (Moscow-Leningrad: gos. izd-vo, 1925), p. 113.

27. Dostoyevskaya, *Vospominaniya A.G. Dostoyevskoy* p. 185. These
renewed impressions might account for a passage in *A Raw Youth [Podros-
tok]*, published in 1875, in which certain personal memories are compared
to the recollection of literary "stabbing scenes" such as passages from
Shakespeare's *Othello*, of Pushkin's *Eugene Onegin* or "the escaped convict's encounter with a child, a little girl, during a cold night, by the well,
in Victor Hugo's *Les Misérables*; it [such a scene] pierces the heart once
and then leaves a wound forever." F. M. Dostoyevski, *Sobraniye sochineni,*
ed. L.P. Grossman *et al.* (Moscow: Goslitizdat, 1956-58), Vol. VIII, p. 524.

28. Numerous readers of the *Diary of a Writer* wrote to Dostoevsky to
express their thoughts on matters both personal and literary. He either
answered them personally, as in the case of Sofia Yefimovna Lurie, or carried on the controversy in further articles of the *Diary*. See Dolinin's note
to another letter to Mrs. Lurie dated April 16, 1876 in Vol. III, pp. 359-60.

29. In fact, the two works had appeared at an interval of four years—
1862 and 1866. It is noteworthy that Dostoevsky in retrospect reduces the
lapse of time.

30. Although he "disagreed" with Tyutchev (1803-1873), Dostoevsky
obviously enjoyed recalling this comparison in his favor. Reference to it
had already appeared in a previous letter, dated April 9, 1876, to a Mrs.
Alshchevskaya. This letter illustrates his view that the creative writer
"should know reality in its minutest details":

Victor Hugo, whom I regard highly as a novelist [for this opinion of
mine, mind you, the late I. Tyutchev got angry with me and said that
Crime and Punishment (my novel) was superior to *Les Misérables*] is
sometimes too lengthy in his use of details, but he has written extraordinary descriptions of which the world would have been deprived had
it not been for him. (Vol. III, p. 206)

31. No such passage is to be found in the published version of the *Diary
of a Writer* for 1876. However, the following thoughts appear in Dostoevsky's notebook for 1875-76:

To F.I. Tyutchev, on the contrary, *Crime and Punishment* seemed superior. I hotly defended my opinion. In Victor Hugo there is an endless
number of artistic mistakes, but that which came out without mistakes
equals Shakespeare at his most lofty.

See *Literaturnoye nasledstvo*, Vol 83 (Moscow, 1971), p. 409. It is likely that Dostoevsky was referring to what he wrote in his notebooks, but did not actually publish in his *Diary*.

32. M. Myriel actually is a bishop at the time the reader meets him.

33. At Dostoevsky's request, this letter was written out in French by his long-time friend, Anna Korvin-Krukovskaya, who had spent a number of years in Paris. See *Pisma*, Vol. IV, note to letter No. 661, p. 380.

34. Dolinin believes that Dostoevsky wrote this letter in the second half of May, 1879, and that the Congress took place in London under Hugo's presidency (p. 380). However, we find no trace of this in the biographical literature on Hugo, an omission difficult to account for since Hugo was 78 at the time and it seems unlikely that his biographers would fail to mention such a trip and such an occasion. On the other hand, Martine Ecalle and Violaine Lumbroso note in their *Album Hugo* ("Bibliothèque de la Pléiade"; Paris: Gallimard, 1964):

> Cependant l'activité publique de Hugo est inlassable. Après avoir prononcé un discours sur Voltaire . . . puis, le 17 Juin 1878, le discours d'ouverture au Congrès littéraire international dont il a été nommé président, il est frappé d'hémiplégie dans la nuit du 20 Juin. (p. 314)

We surmise therefore that Dostoevsky's letter should have been dated May 1878.

35. Standard bibliographies indicate clearly that if Western writers have been challenged to interpret what Dostoevsky said, they have had little inclination to study *how* he said it. Though they have been criticized for their departures, the following noteworthy exceptions to this general rule include Johannes van der Eng's *Dostoevskij romancier: rapports entre sa vision du monde et ses procédés littéraires* (The Hague: Mouton, 1957); and Robert K. Belknap's *The Structure of the Brothers Karamazov* (The Hague: Mouton, 1967), as well as "The Origins of Alëša Karamazov," *American Contributions to the Sixth International Congress of Slavists* (Prague, 1968), ed. William B. Harkins (The Hague: Mouton, 1968), Vol. II, in which Belknap analyzes numerous literary components amalgamated by Dostoevsky to create a new and unique character. Edward Wasiolek discusses problems of composition and structure in the "Introductions" and extensive annotations to his English editions of Dostoevsky's notebooks.

36. Grossman here underlines the similarity between the title of Dostoevsky's first novel *Bednye lyudi* (1846)—which in French translates as *Les Pauvres Gens*—and Hugo's famous poem from his cycle "La Légende des Siècles" (LII) dated February 3, 1854. Grossman is pointing out a *de facto* similarity, not suggesting an influence.

37. Such humanitarian themes were not the prerogative of one writer or country, but were very much in the air in the 1840s. E.g., the works of Eugène Sue (1804-1857), George Sand (1804-1876), or Charles Dickens (1812-1879).

38. Grossman, *op. cit.*, pp. 45-46.

39. In *Literatura i marksizm*, No. 5 (Moscow, 1928), pp. 26-58.

40. Such an affirmation would not withstand a closer analysis. Hugo

might have romanticized the peasantry, but as a Peer of the Realm and an intimate of King Louis-Philippe and his court, he was especially well-informed about the mores of the aristocracy. As deputy-elect to the Legislative Assembly, he took a special interest in the unrest among the working classes and conducted personal inquiries about labor conditions in Parisian factories. See, for example, *Choses vues, Oeuvres complètes de Victor Hugo* ("Edition dite de l'Imprimerie Nationale"; Paris: Librairie Ollendorf-Albin Michel, 1904-1952), Vol. 1, pp.113-125, 212-229; *Actes et Paroles (ibid.)*, Vol. 1, pp. 121-128, 157-165, 346-347.

41. Although Marius's bravery is never to be doubted, it should be pointed out that he left his room not in order to go to the barricades but for a rendezvous with Cosette, with whom he is in love. But Cosette is not to be found—the house is closed, and she and her father have disappeared. As Marius is contemplating suicide, he hears somebody's voice telling him that his friends are awaiting him at the barricades.

42. V.V. Vinogradov, *Evolyutsiya russkogo naturalizma: Gogol i Dostoyevski* (Leningrad: Akademiya, 1929), p. 135.

43. André Maurois, *Olympio, ou la vie de Victor Hugo* (Paris: Hachette, 1954), p. 455.

44. Michael Riffaterre makes the same point with reference to psychological interpretations of literary works:

> . . . ce qui compte en littérature, ce n'est pas tant la psychologie de l'écrivain que ce qu'il en révèle dans son écriture; ce n'est pas tant l'authenticité d'une expérience spirituelle que l'art de convaincre le lecteur qu'elle est réelle, et de la lui faire partager. Ce n'est pas leur vérité, mais leur air de vérité qui fait la valeur de certaines oeuvres d'art. (pp. 226-227)

Michael Riffaterre, "La Vision hallucinatoire chez Victor Hugo," *Modern Language Notes*, Vol. LXXVIII (May, 1963), pp. 225-241. Reprinted in *Essais de stylistique structurale* (Paris: Flammarion, 1971).

45. In this way we hope to avoid the pitfalls of those who, in the words of Rene Wellek:

> . . . conceive of literary study in terms of nineteenth-century positivistic factualism, as a study of sources and influences. They believe in causal explanation, in the illumination which is brought about by tracing motifs, themes, characters, situations, plots, etc., to some other chronologically preceding work. They have accumulated an enormous mass of parallels, similarities, and sometimes identities, but they have rarely asked what these relationships are supposed to show except possibly the fact of one writer's knowledge and reading of another writer. Works of art, however, are not simply sums of sources and influences: they are wholes in which raw materials derived from elsewhere cease to be inert matter and are assimilated into a new structure.

R. Wellek, "The Crisis in Comparative Literature," *Proceedings of the Second International Congress of Comparative Literature*, ed. W.P. Friedrich

(Chapel Hill: University of North Carolina Press, 1959), Vol. I, pp. 149-59. Reprinted in *Concepts of Criticism* (New Haven: Yale University Press, 1963).

Chapter II

1. I wish to acknowledge the work of Scott Andrew Buchan whose writings on the questions discussed in this chapter have been a source of many ideas.

2. Such memorable characters as Luzhin, Marmeladov, Fantine, and Gavroche have been excluded because they can be seen as satellites not indispensable to the basic structure considered here.

3. These omissions particularly concern *Les Misérables*, which is about three times as long as *Crime and Punishment*, owing mainly to the insertion of extensive digressions into the narrative proper. These "parenthèses," as Hugo himself called them, situate Valjean's adventures in a larger social and historical context and emphasize the total time span of the novel. Yet the links between these interruptions of the story and the story itself often are extremely tenuous, structurally speaking, if indeed a connection exists at all.

For example, at the end of an account (in eighteen chapters) of the battle of Waterloo, [*Part Two*, Book One (except for Chap. xix): "Waterloo"] the camp-follower Thénardier appears. As he robs the dead on the dark and deserted battlefield, the hand from which he has taken a ring suddenly moves. In this unexpected fashion Thénardier "rescues" Colonel Pontmercy, thus acquiring rights to Marius Pontmercy's gratitude.

After Valjean and Cosette have hidden in a Parisian convent, Hugo digresses in nineteen chapters on the social, historical, and philosophical significance of monasteries. [*Part Two*, Books Six and Seven: "Le Petit-Picpus" and "Parenthèse."]

Another instance, among others, is Hugo's "History" (in six chapters) of the sewers of Paris—a parenthesis to Valjean's escape from the barricades with the body of Marius. [*Part Five*, Book Two: "L'Intestin du Léviathan."]

The above-mentioned sections, therefore, are neither part of our outline nor will they be further taken into consideration. The same applies to the following parts of *Les Misérables: Part Three*, Books One and Seven, "Paris étudié dans son atome" and "Patron-Minette"; *Part Four*, Books One, Seven, Ten, Eleven, and Twelve (except for Chap. vii), "Quelques pages d'histoire," "L'Argot," "Le 5 Juin 1832," "L'Atome fraternise avec l'ouragan," and "Corinthe."

4. Victor Hugo, *Les Misérables*. Maurice Allem (ed.). "Bibliothèque de la Pléiade." Paris: Gallimard, 1960. Subsequent references to this edition will be indicated by the page number in parenthesis following the quotation.

5. The draft for this letter was found among Dostoevsky's papers. It is not known for certain whether it was ever sent.

6. Vidocq (1775-1857) is probably the best-known exception to this

rule. Thief, adventurer, deserter, condemned to eight years of hard labor for forgery, sent to the galleys at Brest whence he three times escaped, Vidocq became an expert on the mores of the underworld in Paris. In 1809, he offered his services to the Chief of Police of Paris, was made head of a reorganized detective department (with a corps of ex-convicts under his command) and remained in that post for some twenty years. His story (the four volumes of *Mémoires de Vidocq*, allegedly written by Vidocq himself, appeared in 1828), as well as his genius for hunting down criminals, made him a somewhat legendary figure during his own lifetime. This criminal turned defender of the law was the model for Balzac's Vautrin and might well have lent some of his traits to the ex-convict Jean Valjean.

7. In his monumental work, Paul Savey-Casard reports that in 1852 Hugo found the motto that summed up his views on Law and laws: *Pro jure, contra legem*. *Cf*. Paul Savey-Casard, *Le Crime et la peine dans l'oeuvre de Victor Hugo* (Paris: Presses Universitaires de France, 1956), p. 62.

8. Dostoyevski, F.M. *Sobraniye sochineni*. Ed. L.P. Grossman, *et al*. 10 vols. (Moscow: Goslitizda, 1956-1958). Vol. V, p. 550. Subsequent references to Dostoevsky's novels will be taken from this edition and indicated by the volume and page number in parenthesis following the quotation.

9. The semantic resemblances between the quoted passages are indeed striking. A crossroad, physical and mental exhaustion, falling to the ground, heartbreak, tears, and finally kneeling—all are present in both. One should note, however, that Valjean is alone—with himself and with the Bishop's spirit—and that he collapses under the weight of "une puissance invisible." But Raskolnikov, because Sonya's words have found a sudden and overwhelming echo in him, falls to the ground in the midst of a crowd. The difference between the same action being performed in a deserted country spot or in a public square signals the "russification" of Hugo's basic material. This process is further illustrated by Raskolnikov's behavior after he falls to the ground. The concepts of "bowing to the people" as a sign of atonement, of humbling oneself before the common folk as a means of purification, of kissing the earth with "pleasure and happiness" in penance and submission to the source of life, are foreign to both the French Enlightenment and the Church of Rome. On the other hand, they are very much in keeping with Russian orthodox rituals and with a popular tradition which sees self-imposed humiliation and mortification before the humble and the poor as steps on the road to redemption.

10. In this respect both novels fill the conventional structural needs of any detective story.

11. In the Epilogue of the novel there are belated revelations of some of Raskolnikov's selfless deeds—such as being injured in a fire from which he rescued two small children, supporting a dying fellow student out of his own meager resources, etc. . . .

12. I.I. Glivenko, *Iz arkhiva F.M. Dostoyevskogo: Prestupleniye i nakazaniye* (Moscow-Leningrad: Gosizdat, 1931), pp. 168-169.

13. Though Jean Valjean had confessed his "crimes" to Marius, he had kept his good deeds secret. Therefore Marius, who has searched in vain for

the mysterious stranger who rescued him from the barricades, was not only unaware of owing his life to Valjean but, after some investigating, had come to believe that Cosette's adoptive father was a thief, for having robbed Monsieur Madeleine, and a murderer, for having killed Javert. Through Thénardier, who comes to sell him an "extraordinary" secret, Marius learns that Jean Valjean was in fact Monsieur Madeleine, that Javert committed suicide, but that nevertheless the ex-convict is a thief and a murderer. Thénardier's secret is that he had met Valjean carrying a bloody corpse in the sewers, where he himself was hiding. According to him, Valjean had obviously murdered a young man for money and was crossing the sewers to throw the body into the river. This is how Marius, learning the truth about Valjean, comes to fully understand his moral stature.

14. Savey-Casard, *op. cit.,* p. 174.

15. *Ibid.,* p. 178.

16. In her thesis on *Le Gueux chez Victor Hugo* (Paris: Librairie E. Droz, 1936), Maria Ley-Deutsch devotes a very interesting chapter to Thenardier and his family, pp. 256-279.

17. *Ibid.,* p. 273.

18. This vision of "America" is worth quoting in full:

In y a en Amérique dans un pays qui est du côté de Panama, un village appelé la Joya. Ce village se compose d'une seule maison. Une grande maison carrée de trois étages en briques cuites au soleil, chaque côté du carré long de cinq cents pieds, chaque étage en retrait de douze pieds sur l'étage inférieur de façon à laisser devant soi une terrasse qui fait le tour de l'édifice, au centre une cour intérieure où sont les provisions et les munitions, pas de fenêtres, des meurtrières, pas de porte, des échelles, des échelles pour monter du sol à la première terrasse, et de la première à la seconde, et de la seconde à la troisième, des échelles pour descendre dans la cour interiéure, pas de portes aux chambres, des trappes, pas d'escaliers aux chambres, des échelles; le soir on ferme les trappes, on retire les échelles, on braque des tromblons et des carabines aux meurtrières; nul moyen d'entrer; une maison le jour, une citadelle la nuit, huit cents habitants, voilà ce village. Pourquoi tant de précautions? c'est que ce pays est dangereux; il est plein d'anthropophages. Alors pourquoi y va-t-on; c'est que ce pays est merveilleux; on y trouve de l'or. (p. 1462)

19. Svidrigailov was born to Russian society and just spent seven years on his country estate, with plenty of time to read and study. Dostoevsky's readers could easily imagine that Svidrigailov would be acquainted with the literary image of "America," from Chateaubriand forward, as a land where man's natural virtues could flower.

Chapter III

1. *Dnevnik pisatelya za 1876 god* (Paris: YMCA-Press, n.d.), pp. 37-38, 39.

2. *Dostoevsky: Child and Man in His Works* (New York: New York University Press, 1968), pp. 106-107.

3. *The Undiscovered Dostoyevsky* (London: Hamish Hamilton, 1962), p. 176.

4. The association of drunkenness and cruelty was to become, of course, one of the international cliches of Naturalism. It should be enough to recall Zola's *L'Assommoir*, published in 1877, or Jack London's tales of the American North, which appeared a generation later.

5. *Estetika Dostoevskogo* (Berlin: Obelisk, 1923), pp. 95-96.

6. *Nekrasov: l'homme et le poète* (Paris: Université de Paris, 1948).

7. *Ibid.*, p. 273.

8. Corbet's high-handed treatment of Hugo is very much in keeping with an attitude prevalent in French criticism during the first half of this century. Marcel Thiébaut, in his article "Victor Hugo: 1954," describes it in the following terms:

Après avoir fait "tirer" (cas unique) des livres de poésie par centaines de milles, après avoir été vénéré comme un dieu, Hugo a été délaissé, déchiqueté, puis traité de lion empaillé et de simple imbécile. Les symbolistes l'ont dédaigné ou accablé, Gide a prononcé le fameux Hugo, hélas! Les partis en voulant l'utiliser l'ont abaissé. Et puis il y eut un long silence plein d'une distante considération. [*La Revue de Paris*, année 61 (juin, 1954), p. 148]

9. For example, in a book entitled *Witnesses of the Light*, Hugo represents "The Man of Letters" amongst such luminaries as "Dante, the Poet," "Michelangelo, the Artist," "Wagner, the Musician," etc. Washington Gladden, *Witnesses of the Light* (Boston and New York: Houghton, Mifflin, 1903).

10. Ecalle and Lumbroso, *op. cit.*, p. 223.

11. Fernand Gregh, *Victor Hugo: sa vie, son oeuvre* (Paris: Flammarion, 1954), p. 232.

12. "Le succès des *Contemplations . . .* fut prodigieux et la première édition épuisée aussitôt que parue." Maurois, *op. cit.*, p. 425.

13. "Viktor Gyugo i yego russkiye znakomstva: vstrechi; pisma; vospominaniya," *Literaturnoye nasledstvo*, Vols. XXI-XXXII (Moscow, 1937), pp. 777-932.

14. "Smes," *Otechestvennye zapiski*, No. 5, 1856, p. 29. A long and glowing review also appeared in *Otechestvennye zapiski*, No. 8 (1856).

15. Hugo's new book no doubt had a special resonance for Russian readers. In the same issue of *The Contemporary*, a section entitled "Petersburg's Life," devoted to theatrical and meteorological anecdotes and news, ends in the following manner:

The surrounding gardens, the parks and the groves, are becoming greener every day. The nightingales are singing. Summer, at last, has come!
Quand la terre est embaumée
Le coeur de l'homme est meilleur . . . writes Victor Hugo in his

Contemplations [II, XXIII, 3-4] , and this, I believe, is the truth!

Sovremennik, No. 6, 1856, p. 200.

16. "Nekrasov i Viktor Gyugo," in *Russko-yevropeyskiye literaturnye svyazi* (Moscow-Leningrad: Nauka, 1966), pp. 128-136.

17. *Ibid.,* p. 131. It cannot be definitely proved whether Nekrasov knew French or not. Serman says, "Aside from the article published on *Les Contemplations,* Nekrasov could have become acquainted with the book of Hugo's poems with the help of one of his friends." One should also keep in mind, perhaps, that "knowing French" at the time meant knowing it as, say, Turgenev knew French. But even a lesser knowledge would have allowed Nekrasov to read Hugo in the original. Also, the uninterrupted censorship, the long tradition of literary salons and cliques, and the pressures to produce prolifically, all had trained Russian writers to stretch to the utmost a limited command of a language or a limited chance to see a text by means of personal contact with those better informed. Razumikhin actually describes this process in *Crime and Punishment*, when he offers translations from German to Raskolnikov.

18. Such as "Wretched and Elegant" ("Ubogaya i naryadnaya"), "Children's Tears" ("Plach detey"), and "The Thief" ("Vor"), *Ibid.*, pp. 131-132.

19. Victor Hugo, *Oeuvres poétiques*, ed. Pierre Albouy, Tome II ("Bibliothèque de la Pléiade"; Paris: Gallimard, 1967), pp. 572-573.

20. N.A. Nekrasov, *Stikhotvoreniya: 1856-1877,* Vol. II (Moscow, 1948), p. 61.

21. The corresponding lines in Nekrasov, "The horse only sighed deeply,/And looked (as people do submitting to unjust attacks)," also humanize the beast, but they nevertheless remain on a literal level, as is seen, for example, in the substitution of "unjust attack" for "loi formidable."

22. Serman, *op. cit.*, p. 135.

23. *Victor Hugo* (New York: Worthington, 1886), p. 85.
In this instance poetical intuition is corroborated by history. Adèle Hugo, in her *Journal de l'exil*, tells of her father reading "Melancholia" to his family on the 25th of December 1855:

Après nous avoir lu cette pièce, mon père nous dit que c'était elle qui contenait le germe du roman inédit Misérables. . . .

Quoted by Pierre Albouy in his notes to "Melancholia" in *Oeuvres poétiques* op. cit. p. 1458.

24. This quatrain is a parody of the following verses of the French poet Malherbe (1555-1628):

Elle était de ce monde où les plus belles choses
  Ont le pire destin,
Et, rose, elle a vécu ce que vivent les roses,
  L'espace d'un matin.
          (Consolation à M. du Périer.)

25. Some ten months after being abandoned, Fantine decides to go back to her native town of Montreuil-sur-mer. On her way she meets the

family of the innkeeper Thénardier, to whom she entrusts her daughter Cosette for seven francs a month. Arriving alone in Montreuil-sur-mer, she works as a seamstress in a factory for about a year. When her "fault" becomes known, she loses her job and learns "the art of living in misery," sewing 17 hours a day for nine sous. Constantly pressured for money by the Thénardiers, Fantine sells her hair to a barber, her front teeth to a traveling "dentist" and finally, "what is left" to men on the street. A year later, a prostitute and "the specter of herself" at only twenty-five, she dies of consumption and is buried in the pauper's grave.

26. This has been noticed by Pierre Albouy in the following note to "Melancholia":

> Enfin, dans *Les Misérables,* le chapitre, écrit en 1861, où commencent la chute et la passion de Fantine, s'intitule *Mort d'un cheval.* Tandis que Fantine, ses amies et leurs amants déjeunent joyeusement, passe "une jument beauceronne, vieille et maigre et digne de l'équarrisseur" trainant "une charrette fort lourde": elle s'abat et meurt sous les coups. Tholomyès, qui se prépare à abandonner Fantine, trouve là l'occasion d'un calembour; Fantine seule s'apitoie sur la bête, qui préfigure son destin. . . .

Oeuvres poétiques, op. cit., p. 1464.

The treatment meted out to Fantine once she has become a prostitute and belongs to the streets is indeed reminiscent of the cruelty and heartlessness with which the marc has been treated. One winter night, wearing a low-cut evening dress, Fantine paces in front of a cafe full of officers. An idle and warmly dressed gentleman watches her with particular glee:

> Chaque fois que cette femme passait devant lui, il lui jetait, avec une bouffée de la fumée de son cigare, quelque apostrophe qu'il croyait spirituelle et gaie, comme: "Que tu es laide! Veux-tu te cacher! Tu n'as pas de dents!" etc., etc. —Ce monsieur s'appelait M. Bamatabois. La femme, triste spectre paré qui allait et venait sur la neige, ne lui répondait pas, ne le regardait même pas, et n'en accomplissait pas moins en silence et avec une régularité sombre sa promenade qui la ramenait de cinq minutes en cinq minutes sous le sarcasme, comme le soldat condamné qui revient sous les verges. Ce peu d'effet piqua sans doute l'oisif qui, profitant d'un moment où elle se retournait, s'avança derrière elle à pas de loup et en étouffant son rire, se baissa, prit sur le pavé une poignée de neige et la lui plongea brusquement dans le dos entre ses deux épaules nues. (p. 198)

27. This swift narrative tempo—with the exception of the Epilogue, of course—is sustained throughout the novel. In his essay "Dostoevsky in *Crime and Punishment,*" Philip Rahv pinpointed "Dostoevsky's capacity to subdue the time element of the story to his creative purpose. Readers not deliberately attentive to the time-lapse of the action are surprised to learn that its entire span is only two weeks and that of Part I only three days." [Philip Rahv, *The Myth and the Powerhouse* (New York: Farrar, Straus

and Giroux, 1965), p. 108.]

The Idiot (1868) also offers an example of extraordinary narrative pace and manipulation of time. Part I (numbering 202 pages in our Russian edition), in which all the characters and themes of the novel are presented while the action is in constant progress, begins at 9 o'clock one morning and ends late at night on the same day.

28. ". . . a dream might be described as *a substitute for an infantile scene modified by being transferred onto a recent experience*" (p. 585, italics in original). A dream can be inserted into a psychical chain that has to be traced backwards in the memory from a pathological idea (p. 133). ". . . [the] ego may be represented in a dream several times over, now directly and now through identification with extraneous persons"(p. 358). "A dream . . . has no alternative but to represent a wish in the situation of having been fulfilled . . . the mind has wishes at its disposal whose fulfillment produces unpleasure."

Clinical findings and theoretical innovations in psychoanalysis and neurophysiology in the last decade have made the direct application of Freudian theory to literature a somewhat dubious enterprise. It is interesting, nonetheless, how two men of such different backgrounds and disciplines arrived at almost identical perceptions. See Freud, *The Interpretation of Dreams* (New York: Avon Books, 1968), originally published as *Die Traumdeutung* in 1899. See also an article by Ruth Mortimer, "Dostoevski and the Dream," *Modern Philology*, Vol. LIV (November, 1956), pp. 106-116.

29. Mortimer, *op. cit.*, p. 110.

30. Raskolnikov calls a policeman and gives him money to take the girl home in order to protect her from a "gentleman" who had been watching her with excessive interest. He then tells the startled policeman, "What is it to you? Drop it! Let him amuse himself."

31. It is noteworthy that Dunya's sacrifice would put her brother in the role of a dependent child.

32. Mortimer, *op. cit.*, pp. 109-110, writes: "In the prolonged struggle of the mare is dramatized the senseless suffering and the strange endurance under that suffering of women like Sonya."

33. Darya Franzovna of course being the procuress who had approached Sonya Marmeladov.

34. W.D. Snodgrass, in his article "Crime for Punishment: The Tenor of Part One" [*Hudson Review*, Vol. XIII, No. 2 (1960), pp. 202-253] makes a detailed analysis of the mare-beating dream. Though a pioneering contribution filled with many new insights, the Snodgrass article is marred by excessive attribution of symbolic associations. For example, since, "all the characters in the dream are the dreamer," Raskolnikov is "the horse, the little boy, the father [and] the brute Mikolka"(p. 239). The horse, in turn, represents "the teenaged girls, Dunya and Sonya [and] the pawnbroker, the landlady and the mother [and] Marmeladov and Raskolnikov"(p. 239).

Another instance of Snodgrass's making interpretations at all costs is his statement that: "We should notice the great emphasis upon beating the horse across the eyes; Raskolnikov feels particularly guilty about his mother's knitting shawls and cuffs at night; he fears she may go blind before he can help her"(p. 234).

35. *Dnevnik pisatelya za 1877 god, op. cit.*, p. 402.

36. See for example letter of February 22, 1854, and of March 27, 1854 in *Pisma*, Vol. I, pp. 138, 139, 145.

37. Attested by Wrangel in his "Recollections on Dostoyevski in Siberia" ("Vospominaniya o F.M. Dostoyevskom v Sibiri"), *F.M. Dostoyevski v vospominaniyakh sovremennikov, op. cit.*, Vol. I, p. 250.

38. Scholarly investigations have shown that although "Melancholia" is dated July 1838, it was in fact begun in 1846 and completed in 1855. Writing in exile, Hugo added stanzas six, seven and eight, in which a departure from typically romantic attitudes can be observed. The first added episode was the story of the horse, which attracted attention and praise immediately upon publication. This episode is considered as one of the first expressions of Hugo's "universal pity," which engulfs not only social victims but all living creatures, and of the metaphysical problems posed by their sufferings. See Victor Hugo, *Les Contemplations*, ed. Joseph Vianey (Paris: Librairie Hachette, 1922), Vol. II, pp. 111-117; and *Oeuvres poetiques, op. cit.*, p. 1463.

39. André Maurois, *op. cit.*, p. 536.

40. One must also take into account that Dostoevsky had certainly not forgotten the 20-page obituary of Nekrasov he had included in his *Diary* for December 1877. There we read in the last paragraph: "Nekrasov is a Russian historical type, one of the major examples of the contradictions and duality, in the field of morals and convictions, of which Russians are capable in our sad transitional time." *Dnevnik pisatelya za 1877 god, op. cit.*, p. 489.

Chapter IV

1. Our purpose is not to investigate Raskolnikov's dreams *per se*, but to trace how material from some of Hugo's work made its way into Dostoevsky's text. We have found no relevant sources for Raskolnikov's second and fourth dreams and therefore we will not include them in the present study.

2. *Victor Hugo raconté par un témoin de sa vie, Oeuvres complètes de Victor Hugo, op. cit.*, Chap. 1, p. 246.

3. ". . . ce que j'écrirai ainsi ne sera peut-être pas inutile. Ce journal de mes souffrances, heure par heure, minute par minute, supplice par supplice, si j'ai la force de le mener jusqu'au moment où il me sera *physiquement* impossible de continuer, cette histoire, nécéssairement inachevée, mais aussi complète que possible, de mes sensations, ne portera-t-elle point avec elle un grand et profond enseignement?" *Le Dernier Jour d'un condamné, Ibid.*, Vol. II, chap. vi, p. 337.

4. ". . . Moi, misérable qui ai commis un véritable crime, qui ai versé le sang!" *Ibid.*, chap. xi, p. 347.

5. Here is how chapter xlvii reads:

MON HISTOIRE
Note de l'éditeur. —On n'a pu encore retrouver les feuillets qui se rattachaient à celui-ci. Peut-être, comme ceux qui suivent semblent l'indiquer, le condamné n'a-t-il pas eu le temps de les écrire. Il était tard quand cette pensée lui est venue.

Ibid., chap. xlvii, p. 442.

6. This intentional vagueness strengthens the polemical aspect of the work. The resulting "mystery" was not to everybody's taste, as is shown in the following passage from *Victor Hugo raconté par un témoin de sa vie,* (*op. cit.,* Chap. I, p. 247), where the publisher's reaction is described:

Quand il en fut au passage où l'auteur, voulant que son condamné reste absolument impersonnel afin de ne pas intéresser à un condamne spécial, mais à tous, suppose que les feuillets qui contenaient l'histoire de sa vie ont été perdus, M. Gosselin lui conseilla, dans l'intérêt de la vente du livre, "de retrouver les feuillets perdus." M. Victor Hugo répondit qu'il avait pris M. Gosselin pour éditeur et non pour collaborateur.

7. Hugo, *Le Dernier Jour d'un condamné, op. cit.,* chap. xlii, pp. 431-434.

8. *Hugo: l'homme et l'oeuvre* (Paris: Hatier, 1952), p. 53.

9. Vissarion Belinsky, for example, wrote that "Hugo had never been condemned to the death penalty, but what horrible, heart-rending truth [appears] in his *Dernier Jour*." Quoted by Vinogradov, *op. cit.,* p. 130.

Belinsky was not alone in admiring Hugo's short novel. At the end of April 1830, Alexander Pushkin was writing in his own beautiful French to Princess Vera Fedorovna Vyazemskaya, "Vous avez raison de trouver *l'Ane* délicieux. C'est un des ouvrages les plus marquants du moment. On l'attribute à V. Hugo—j'y vois plus de talent, que dans *Le Dernier Jour* ou il y en beaucoup." [Quoted by Vinogradov, *op. cit.,* p. 129] Pushkin, of course, had erred in attributing to Hugo a book published by a literary rival in the same year (1829). *L'Ane mort et la femme guillotinée* was, in fact, the creation of Jules Janin (1804-1874). Although Pushkin was mistaken as to who had written *L'Ane*, he seems to have been quite positive about the authorship of *Le Dernier Jour*, which had first appeared in Russian as early as 1830. [Vinogradov, *op. cit.,* p. 141, fn.] At any rate, all doubts were dispelled when Hugo, who had originally published the book unsigned in February 1829, definitely acknowledged his authorship in a forceful preface written for the new edition of March 1832: "En 1832, il ajoutait au *Dernier Jour d'un condamné*, une préface considérable qui prenait par le raisonnement la question que le livre avait prise par l'émotion et qui plaidait devant l'esprit ce qu'il avait plaidé devant le coeur." *Victor Hugo raconté par un témoin de sa vie, op. cit.,* chap. li, p. 248.

10. See Victor Brombert's superb article, "Prison de la pensée: Le condamné de Hugo." *L'Arc,* 57 (1974). See also Joseph Frank's *Dostoevsky. op. cit.,* p. 109.

11. See letter of August 9, 1838, in *Pisma,* Vol. I, p. 47.

12. It has become customary to look upon these accounts as exactly autobiographical. Both Magarshak and Robert Lord, for example, see in them a faithful rendering of the mock execution Dostoevsky endured on the morning of December 22nd, 1849. "He gave a full description both of the scene and of what he felt at the time in *The Idiot*," writes Magarshak. (*Dostoevsky, op. cit.*, p. 124.) "There exist several eyewitness accounts of the scene so laboriously acted out on that snowbound square in Petersburg. The best account of all, though, is that of Prince Myshkin in *The Idiot*. The account is simply a dramatization . . . of the scene. . . ." (Robert Lord, *Dostoevsky: Essays and Perspectives* [Berkeley and Los Angeles: University of California Press, 1970], p. 15.

Although he devotes an entire chapter to the study of the "condemned man" in *The Idiot*, Richard Peace follows the same patterns of literary attribution:

> Thus the existence of the condemned man haunts the novel almost from its opening pages; and in the ensuing scene with the Yepanchin sisters the theme is taken up again and further developed. Here Myshkin dwells on the state of mind of the condemned man. . . . In this account of the man reprieved at the very last moment, Dostoevsky is, in fact, describing his own experiences.

See R. Pease, *Dostoevsky. An Examination of the Major Novels* (Cambridge: Cambridge University Press, 1971), pp. 120-21. The wish for a more discerning interpretation is at last fulfilled by Larry R. Andrews, "Dostoevskij and Hugo's Le Dernier Jour d'un condamné," *Comparative Literature*, Vol. XXIX, No. 1 (Winter 1977), pp. 1-16. In this thoughtful contribution, which appeared as the present volume goes to press, Andrews gives due to the "remarkable connections between Hugo's *Le Dernier Jour d'un condamné* and Dostoevskij's works, which seem to bear out the intuitive insight of recent critics who compare the modernity of the two writers"(p. 16).

13. Such as, for example, the description of the prisoner being driven through the town to the scaffold. In *The Idiot*: "All round him there were crowds of people yelling, shouting, ten thousand faces, ten thousand eyes—and all this had to be endured. . ."(p. 75). In *Le Dernier Jour d'un condamné*: "Et la charrette allait, allait, et les boutiques passaient, et les enseignes se succédaient, écrites, peintes, dorées, et la populace riait et trépignait dans la boue, et je me laissais aller, comme à leurs rêves ceux qui sont endormis"(p. 450).

14. Vinogradov, *op. cit.*, pp. 127-152.

15. *Ibid.*, p. 149.

16. *Dnevnik pistelya za 1876 god, op. cit.*, pp. 414-415.

17. *Op. cit.*, p. 150.

18. *Ibid.*, p. 152.

19. Although the reader is unaware of the topic discussed, it could be interpreted as sinister—a plot, perhaps, or the planning of a crime.

20. There is perhaps another difference here—a difference in mood. The silence Raskolnikov experiences is due to the death of those who used to

live in this "same" apartment, and therefore it is frightening. For the condemned man the silence, which otherwise would be normal at such a time and place, makes frightening the noises which were heard before. Moreover, the reference to the immobility of the portraits is unsettling for it seems to suggest that the condemned man thought for an instant that these portraits might have lived their own spectral life.

21. This particular expression of Dostoevsky's symbolism has been noted by P.M. Bitsilli. In a highly original study on the nature of the Dostoevskian novel, Bitsilli writes that:

> The most terrifying scenes [in Dostoevsky's novels] very frequently take place on a staircase. . . . It does not matter by virtue of what associations the image of the staircase became fixed in its symbolic meaning in the author's mind. This image—at least in Dostoevsky—is the image of a narrow, dirty, dark, winding staircase which it is so difficult to climb, on which it is so easy to slip and fall down the steps, where it is so easy to waylay someone—serves all by itself as the ultimately expressive symbol of the tormented and "grievous" mental processes of all his heroes.

P.M. Bitsilli, "On the Inner Form of the Dostoevskian Novel" ("K voprosu o vnutrennei forme roman Dostoyevskogo"), Sofiya Universitet, Istorikofilologicheski fakultet, *Godishnik*, Vol. XLII (1945-46), pp. 1-71; reprinted in D. Fanger, ed., *O Dostoyevskom; Stati* ("Brown University Slavic Reprint Series IV"; Providence, R.I.: Brown University Press, 1966), pp. 53, 55.

In this particular instance, once could interpret Raskolnikov's climbing the staircase as symbolic of the progressive estrangement from the world which led to his total alienation. By the time he reaches the second floor, he finds himself completely alone and crossing back into his "familiar" obsession. On the fourth floor he will confront this obsession and be defeated by it. When attempting to retreat, he will learn that all exits are now blocked and that the outside world has caught up with him.

22. There is also the fact that as an ex-convict he was required to report regularly to the police, instead of vanishing by assuming a new identity.

23. One notes a number of resemblances between Valjean's and the condemned man's dreams; for example, first person account, quest, unanswered questions, meeting death in disguise, etc.

24. Anne Ubersfeld's "Le Rêve de Jean Valjean" *L'Arc (op. cit.,* pp. 41-50) is an interesting psychoanalytical decoding of the events of the dream in terms of what she calls Hugo's "classical obsessional neurosis."

Chapter V

1. Belknap, "The Origins of Alesa Kramazov," *op. cit.*, p. 16.

2. *Ibid.*, p. 8. "Mixail" is a story by Anna Korvin-Krukovskaya published in *Epokha* in 1874.

3. *Choses vues, Oeuvres complètes de Victor Hugo* ("Edition dite de l'Imprimerie Nationale"; Paris: Librairie Ollendorf-Albin Michel, 1904-

1952), Vol. I, p. 60.
4. The end of the scene reads as follows:

"Il n'y qu'un cas, monsieur, où je pourrais arrêter la chose, ce serait celui ou vous signeriez votre déposition; le voulez-vous?"
"Si la liberté de cette femme tient à ma signature, la voici."
Et V.H. signa.
La femme ne cessait de dire: "Dieu! que ce monsieur est bon! Mon Dieu, qu'il est donc bon!"
Ces malheureuses femmes ne sont pas seulement étonnées et reconnaissantes quand on est compatissant envers elles; elles ne le sont pas moins quand on est juste.

Ibid., p. 62.
5. *Istoricheski Vestnik* (February, 1904), pp. 448-542.
6. *Ibid.*, pp. 519-520. The tone, the manner of speech, and the formulation of ideas in the above passage seem to vouch for the accuracy of Mrs. Pochinkovskaya's memory.
7. It is remarkable that Dostoevsky apparently feels no need to "imagine" how the streetwalker might have reacted or felt at being spat on by three men—perhaps because this can quite easily be guessed on the basis of stereotyped thinking, or perhaps because it is more interesting to invent a more unusual situation.
8. See Belknap, "The Origins of Alëša Karamazov," *op. cit.*, p. 15: "The redistribution of attributes into related characters, taken together with the transformation of figures of speech, allows Dostoevskij to borrow extensively without producing characters identical to their sources."
9. See Bem, "Hugo and Dostoevsky," *op. cit.*, pp. 76, 79.

SELECTED BIBLIOGRAPHY

Alekseyev, M.P. "Viktor Gyugo i yego russkiye znakomstva: vstrechi; pisma; vospominaniya," *Literaturnoye nasledstvo*, Vols. XXXI-XXXII (Moscow, 1937), pp. 777-932.

Andrews, Larry R. "Dostoevskij and Hugo's *Le Dernier Jour d'un Condamné*," in *Comparative Literature*, Vol. XXIX (Winter 1977), Number 1.

Angrand, Pierre. "Javert jaugé, jugé," *Mercure de France*, Vol. CCCXLIV (April, 1962), pp. 815-38.

Arban, Dominique. *Les années d'apprentissage de Fiodor Dostoievski*. Paris: Payot, 1968.

Bailbé, Joseph Marc, *et al.* "Jules Janin et le Romantisme," in *Jules Janin et son temps: Un moment du Romantisme*. Paris: Presses Universitaires de France, 1974.

Bakhtin, M.M. *Problemy tvorchestva Dostoyevskogo*. Leningrad: Priboy, 1929. Second edition, Moscow, 1963.

Barrère, Jean Bertrand. *La fantaisie de Victor Hugo*. Vol. I: 1802-1851. Vol. II: 1852-1885. Paris: J. Corti, 1949 and 1960.

Barrère, Jean Bertrand. *Hugo: l'homme et l'oeuvre*. Paris: Hatier, 1952.

Baudouin, Charles. *Psychanalyse de Victor Hugo*. Genève: Editions du Mont-Blanc, 1943.

Belchikov, N.F. *Dostoyevski v protsesse Petrashevtsev*. Moscow-Leningrad: 1936.

Belknap, Robert L. *The Structure of The Brothers Karamazov*. The Hague: Mouton, 1967.

Belknap, Robert L. "The Origins of Alëša Karamazov," *American Contributions to the Sixth International Congress of Slavists* (Prague, 1968). Vol. II: *Literary Contributions*. Ed. William E. Harkins. The Hague: Mouton, 1968.

Bellessort, André. *Victor Hugo: essai sur son oeuvre*. Paris: Perrin et Cie, Libraires-Editeurs, 1930.

Bem, A.L., ed. *O Dostoyevskom*. 3 vols. Prague: Petropolis, 1929-1936.

Bem, A.L. "Gyugo i Dostoyevski," *Slavia* (Prague), Vol. XV (1937-1938), pp. 73-86.

Bem, A.L. *Dostoyevski: psikhoanaliticheskiye etyudy*. Prague: Petropolis, 1938.

Benoit-Lévy, Edmond. *Les Misérables de Victor Hugo*. ("Société française d'éditions littéraires et techniques.") Paris: Edgar Malfère, 1929.

Berret, Paul. "Victor Hugo et la vie future," *Revue des deux mondes*, 8ᵉ série, Vol. XXVII (May 15, 1935), pp. 345-57.

Bersaucourt, Albert de. *Les pamphlets contre Victor Hugo*. Paris: Mercure de France, 1912.

Biré, Edmond. *Victor Hugo après 1830*. 2 vols. ("Librairie Académique Didier.") Paris: Perrin et Cie, Libraires-Editeurs, 1891.

Bitsilli, Pyotr Mikhailovich. "K voprosu o vnutrenney forme romana Dostoyevskogo," Sofiya Universitet, Istorikofilologicheski fakultet, *Godishnik*, Vol. XLII (1945-1946), pp. 1-71. (Reprinted in Fanger, Donald, ed., *O Dostoyevskom: Stati*. ("Brown University Slavic Reprint Series IV.") Providence, R.I.: Brown University Press, 1966.)

Brochu, André. *Hugo: Amour/Crime/Révolution*. Montréal: Presses de l'Université de Montréal, 1974.

Brodski, N.L., ed. *Tvorcheski put Dostoyevskogo*. Leningrad, 1924.

Brombert, Victor. "Victor Hugo: la prison et l'espace," *Revue des sciences humaines*, Fasc. CXVII (Janvier-Mars, 1965), pp. 59-79.

Brombert, Victor. "Prison de la pensée: Le condamné de Hugo," *L'Arc*, 57 (Revue trimestrielle, 1974).

Butor, Michel. "Victor Hugo romancier," *Tel Quel*, Vol. V (Winter, 1964), pp. 60-77.

Carr, Edward Hallett. *Dostoevsky: 1821-1881*. London: Allen and Unwin, 1931.

Catteau, Jacques, ed. *Dostoievski*. Cahiers de l'Herne, 24; Série Slave. Paris: Editions de l'Herné, 1973.

Chulkov, Georgi. *Kak robotal Dostoyevski.* Moscow, 1939.

Corbet, Charles. *Nekrasov: l'homme et le poète.* Paris: Université de Paris, 1948.

de Jonge, Alex. *Dostoevsky and the Age of Intensity.* London: Secker and Warburg, 1975.

Dolinin, A.S., ed. *F.M. Dostoyevski: stati i materialy.* 2 vols. St. Petersburg: 1922. Leningrad: Mysl, 1925.

Dolinin, A.S., ed. *F.M. Dostoyevski: materialy i issledovaniya.* Leningrad: Izd-vo Akademii nauk SSSR, 1935.

Dolinin, A.S., ed. *F.M. Dostoyevski v vospominaniyakh sovremennikov.* 2 vols. Moscow, 1964.

Dolinin, A.S. [Iskoz, Arkadi Semenovich], ed. *F.M. Dostoyevski: bibliografiya proizvedeni F.M. Dostoyevskogo i literatury o nyom.* Moscow, 1968.

Dostoevsky, Fyodor. *Crime and Punishment.* Trans. Jessie Coulson. Ed. George Gibian. New York: W.W. Norton, 1964.

Dostoevsky, Fyodor. *Dostoevsky's Occasional Writings.* Ed. and trans. David Magarshack. New York: Random House, 1963.

Dostoevsky, Fyodor. *The Notebooks for Crime and Punishment.* Ed. and trans. Edward Wasiolek. Chicago: University of Chicago Press, 1967.

Dostoevsky, Fyodor: *The Notebooks for The Idiot.* Trans. Katherine Strelsky. Ed. Edward Wasiolek. Chicago: University of Chicago Press, 1967.

Dostoevsky, Fyodor. *The Notebooks for The Possessed.* Trans. Katherine Strelsky. Ed. Edward Wasiolek. Chicago: University of Chicago Press, 1968.

Dostoevsky, Fyodor. *The Notebooks for A Raw Youth.* Trans. Victor Terras. Ed. Edward Wasiolek. Chicago: University of Chicago Press, 1969.

Dostoievski, F.M. *Crime et châtiment.* Traduction, introduction, notes, bibliographie par Pierre Pascal. Paris: Editions Garnier Frères, 1961.

Dostoievski, F.M. *Récits de la maison des morts.* Traduction, introduction, notes, bibliographie par Pierre Pascal. Paris: Editions Garnier Frères, 1961.

Dostoyevskaya, A.G. *Dnevnik A.G. Dostoyevskoy: 1867 goda.* Moscow, 1923.

Dostoyevskaya, A.G. *Vospominaniya A.G. Dostoyevskoy*. Ed. L. P. Grossman. Moscow-Leningrad: Gos. Izd-vo, 1925.

Dostoyevski, F.M. *Pisma*. Ed. A.S. Dolinin. 4 vols. Moscow-Leningrad: Goslitizdat, 1928-1959.

Dostoyevski, F.M. *Sobraniye sochineni*. Ed. L.P. Grossman, *et al.* 10 vols. Moscow: Goslitizdat, 1956-1959.

Dostoyevski, F.M. *Neizdannyi Dostoyevski*. Ed. L.M. Rozenblum, *et al. Literaturnoye nasledstvo*, Vol. 83. Moscow: Izd-vo Nauka, 1971.

Dostoyevski, F.M. *Novye materialy; issledovanniya*. Ed. L.M. Rozenblum, *et al. Literaturnoye nasledstvo*, Vol. 86. Moscow: Izd-vo Nauka, 1973.

Dostoyevski, F.M. *Dnevnik pisatelya*. 3 vols. Paris: YMCA-Press, n.d.

Ecalle, Martine and Lumbroso, Violaine. *Album Hugo: iconographie réunie et commentée*. ("Bibliothèque de la Pléiade.") Paris: Gallimard, 1964.

Emery, Léon. *Victor Hugo en son siècle*. Lyon: Les Cahiers libres, 1962.

Eng, Johannes van der. *Dostoevskij romancier: rapports entre sa vision du monde et ses procédés littéraires*. The Hague: Mouton, 1957.

Escholier, Raymond. *Victor Hugo: artiste*. Paris: Editions G. Crès, 1926.

Escholier, Raymond. *Hugo: roi de son siècle*. Paris: Arthaud, 1970.

Etiemble, René. *Comparaison n'est pas raison; la crise de la littérature comparée*. Paris: Gallimard, 1963.

Evdokimoff, Paul. *Dostoievsky et le problème du mal*. ("Collection Ondes.") Lyon: Editions du Livre Français, 1942.

Fanger, Donald. *Dostoevsky and Romantic Realism*. Cambridge, Massachusetts: Harvard University Press, 1965.

Frank, Joseph. *Dostoevsky: The Seeds of Revolt, 1821-1849*. Princeton, N.J.: Princeton University Press, 1976.

Freud, Sigmund. *The Interpretation of Dreams*. New York: Avon Books, 1968.

Gide, André. *Dostoievsky*. Paris: Plon, 1923.

Girard, René. *Dostoievski, du double à l'unité*. Paris: Plon, 1963.

174

Gladden, Washington. *Witnesses of the Light.* New York: Houghton, Mifflin, 1903.

Glivenko, I.I., ed. *Iz arkhiva F.M. Dostoyevskogo: Prestupleniye i nakazaniye; neizdanniye materialy.* Moscow-Leningrad: Gosizdat, 1931.

Grant, Elliott M. *Victor Hugo: A Select and Critical Bibliography.* Chapel Hill: University of North Carolina Press, 1966.

Grant, Richard B. *The Perilous Quest: Image, Myth, and Prophecy in the Narratives of Victor Hugo.* Durham, N.C.: Duke University Press, 1968.

Gregh, Fernand. *Victor Hugo: sa vie, son oeuvre.* Paris: Flammarion, 1954.

Grossman, Leonid Petrovich. *Seminari po Dostoyevskomu.* Moscow-Petrograd: Gos. Izd-vo, 1922.

Grossman, Leonid Petrovich. *Tvorchestvo, Poetika, Put.* 3 vols. in *Tvorchestvo Dostoyevskogo.* Moscow: Sovremennye problemy, 1928.

Guardini, Romano. *L'univers religieux de Dostoievski.* Tr. Henri Engelmann and Robert Givord. ("Collection Esprit: la condition humaine.") Paris: Editions du Seuil, 1947.

Guyard, Marius-François. *La littérature comparée.* Paris: Presses Universitaires de France, 1965.

Guyer, Foster Erwin. *The Titan: Victor Hugo.* New York: S.F. Vanni, 1955.

Hamelin, Jacques. *Les plaidoiries de Victor Hugo.* Paris: Librairie Hachette, 1935.

Heugel, Jacques. *Essai sur la philosophie de Victor Hugo, du point de vue gnostique.* Paris: Calmann-Levy, 1922.

Hingley, Ronald. *The Undiscovered Dostoyevsky.* London: Hamish Hamilton, 1962.

Hugo, Victor. *Oeuvres complètes de Victor Hugo.* (Ne varietur.) 48 vols. Paris: Hetzel, Quantin, 1880-1889.

Hugo, Victor. *Oeuvres complètes de Victor Hugo.* Ed. Paul Meurice, Gustave Simon, and Cécile Daubray. 45 vols. ("Edition dite de l'Imprimerie Nationale.") Paris: Librairie Ollendorff-Albin Michel, 1904-1952.

Hugo, Victor. *Les Contemplations.* Ed. Joseph Vianey. 3 vols.

Paris: Librairie Hachette, 1922.

Hugo, Victor. *Claude Gueux*. Edition critique présentée par P. Savey-Casard. Paris: Presses Universitaires de France, 1956.

Hugo, Victor. *Les Misérables*. Ed. Maurice Allem. ("Bibliothèque de la Pléiade.") Paris: Gallimard, 1960.

Hugo, Victor. *Promontorium Somnii*. Ed. René Journet and Guy Robert. ("Collection 'Annales de Besançon'," Vol. XLII.) Paris: Les Belles Lettres, 1961.

Hugo, Victor. *Oeuvres poétiques*. Ed. Pierre Albouy. 2 vols. ("Bibliothèque de la Pléiade.") Paris: Gallimard, 1964-1967.

Hugo, Victor. *Un carnet des Misérables: octobre-décembre, 1860*. Ed. Jean-Bertrand Barrère. Paris: Minard, Lettres Modernes, 1965.

Ikor, Roger. "Le romancier populaïre," chap. v in *Victor Hugo*. ("Collection Génies et Réalités.") Paris: Librairie Hachette, 1967.

Istoricheski vestnik, February, 1904.

Jackson, Robert Louis. *Dostoevsky's Quest for Form: A Study of His Philosophy of Art*. New Haven: Yale University Press, 1966.

Joussain, André. *L'esthétique de Victor Hugo: le pittoresque dans le lyrisme et dans l'épopée*. ("Société Française d'Imprimerie et de Librairie.") Paris: Boivin et Cie, 1920.

Komarovich, V. "Peterburgskiye felyetony Dostoyevskogo," *Felyetony sorokovykh godov*. Ed. Yu. Oksman. Moscow-Leningrad: Akademiya, 1930, pp. 89-126.

Komarovich, V. "Mirovaya garmoniya Dostoyevskogo," pp. 117-149, and "Yunost Dostoyevskogo," pp. 73-115, *O Dostoyevskom: Stati*. Ed. Donald Fanger. ("Brown University Slavic Reprint Series IV.") Providence, R.I.: Brown University Press, 1966.

Kosta, Edmund K. *Schiller in Russian Literature*. Philadelphia: University of Pennsylvania Press, 1965.

Lapshin, I.I. *Estetika Dostoyevskogo*. Berlin: Obelisk, 1923.

Lary, N.M. *Dostoevsky and Dickens: A Study of Literary Influence*. London and Boston: Routledge and Kegan Paul, 1973.

Lavrin, Janko. *Dostoevsky: A Study*. London: Methuen, 1943.

176

Levaillant, Maurice. *La crise mystique de Victor Hugo: 1843-1856*. Paris: Librairie José Corti, 1954.

Levinson, André. *La vie pathétique de Dostoievski*. Paris: Plon, 1931.

Ley-Deutsch, Maria. *Le gueux chez Victor Hugo*. Paris: Librairie E. Droz, 1936.

Leykina-Svirskaya, Vera Romanovna. *Petrashevtsy*. Moscow, 1965.

Lord, Robert. *Dostoevsky: Essays and Perspectives*. Berkeley and Los Angeles: University of California Press, 1970.

Magarshack, David. *Dostoevsky*. New York: Harcourt, Brace, and World, 1961.

Martinet, André. "Structure and Language," tr. Thomas G. Penchoen, *Structuralism*. Vols. XXXVI-XXXVII. Ed. Jacques Ehrmann. ("Yale French Studies.") New Haven: Yale University Press, 1966, pp. 10-18.

Masaryk, T.G. *The Spirit of Russia*. Tr. Robert Bass. Ed. George Gibian. New York: Barnes and Noble, 1967.

Maurois, André. *Olympio, ou la vie de Victor Hugo*. Paris: Librairie Hachette, 1954.

Mochulski, Konstantin. *Dostoyevski: zhizn i tvorchestvo*. Paris: YMCA–Press, 1947.

Mortimer, Ruth. "Dostoevski and the Dream," *Modern Philology*, Vol. LIV (November, 1956), pp. 106-116.

Murry, J. Middleton. *Fyodor Dostoevsky: A Critical Study*. New York: Russell & Russell, 1966. First printed in 1924.

Nekrasov, Nikolai Alekseevich. *Stikhotvoreniya: 1856-1877*. Moscow, 1948.

Nettement, Alfred. *Etudes critiques sur le feuilleton-roman*. 2 vols. Paris: Librairie de Perrodil, 1845-1846.

Nisard, Désiré. *Essais sur l'école romantique*. ("Librairie Nouvelle.") Paris: Calmann-Lévy, 1889.

Otechestvennye zapiski, Nos. 5 and 8 (1856).

Pachmuss, Temira. *F.M. Dostoevsky: Dualism and Synthesis of the Human Soul*. Carbondale: Southern Illinois University Press, 1963.

Pascal, Pierre. *Dostoievsky: l'homme et l'oeuvre*. Lausanne:

Editions l'Age d'homme, 1970.

Passage, Charles E. *Dostoevski the Adapter: A Study in Dostoevski's Use of the Tales of Hoffman.* Chapel Hill: University of North Carolina Press, 1954.

Peace, Richard. *Dostoyevsky: An Examination of the Major Novels.* Cambridge: Cambridge University Press, 1971.

Peyre, Henri. *French Literary Imagination and Dostoevsky, and Other Essays.* Tuscaloosa: University of Alabama Press, 1975.

Praz, Mario. *The Romantic Agony.* New York: Meridian Books, 1956.

Proffer, Carl R., ed. *The Unpublished Dostoevsky: Diaries and Notebooks, 1860-1881.* 3 vols. Ann Arbor: Ardis, 1973, 1975, 1976.

Rahv, Philip. *The Myth and the Powerhouse.* New York: Farrar, Straus and Giroux, 1965.

Reeve, F.D. *The Russian Novel.* New York: McGraw-Hill, 1966.

Ricatte, R. "Sur *Les Misérables:* le moraliste et ses personnages," *Mercure de France,* Vol. CCCXLII (May, 1961), pp. 48-65.

Riffaterre, Michael. "Victor Hugo, Critic of Shakespeare," *The American Society Legion of Honor Magazine,* Vol. XXXI, No. 3 (1960), pp. 139-152.

Riffaterre, Michael. "Victor Hugo's Poetics," *The American Society Legion of Honor Magazine,* Vol. XXXII, No. 3 (1961), pp. 181-196.

Riffaterre, Michael. *Essais de stylistique structurale.* Paris: Flammarion, 1971.

Rowe, William Woodin. *Dostoevsky: Child and Man in His Works.* New York: New York University Press, 1968.

Rudwin, Maximilien. *Satan et le satanisme dans l'oeuvre de Victor Hugo.* Paris: Les Belles Lettres, 1926.

Sarraute, Nathalie. *L'ère du soupçon. Essais sur le roman.* Paris: Gallimard, 1956.

Savey-Casard, Paul. *Le crime et la peine dans l'oeuvre de Victor Hugo.* Paris: Presses Universitaires de France, 1956.

Savey-Casard, Paul. "L'évolution démocratique de Victor Hugo," *Revue d'Histoire Littéraire de la France,* Vol. LX (Juillet-

Septembre, 1960), pp. 316-333.

Seduro, Vladimir. *Dostoyevski in Russian Literary Criticism: 1846-1956.* New York: Columbia University Press, 1957.

Seduro, Vladimir. "Les récents développements des études sur Dostoievsky en Union Soviétique: 1955-1960," *Problèmes soviétiques,* No. 3 (1960).

Seduro, Vladimir. *Dostoevski's Image in Russia Today.* Belmont, Massachusetts: Nordland, 1975.

Serman, I.Z. "Nekrasov i Viktor Gyugo," *Russko-yevropeyskiye literaturnye svyazi.* Moscow-Leningrad: Nauka, 1966, pp. 128-136.

Shaw, Joseph T. "Literary Indebtedness and Comparative Literary Studies," *Comparative Literature: Method and Perspective.* Ed. Horst Frenz and Newton P. Stallknecht. Carbondale: Southern Illinois University Press, 1961, pp. 58-71.

Snodgrass, W.E. "Crime for Punishment: The Tenor of Part One," *Hudson Review,* Vol. XIII, No. 2 (1960), pp. 202-253.

Sovremennik, No. 6 (1856).

Swinburne, Algernon Charles. *Victor Hugo.* New York: Worthington, 1886.

Thiébaut, Marcel. "Victor Hugo: 1954," *La Revue de Paris,* Année 61 (Juin, 1954), pp. 140-152.

Trousson, Raymond. *Un problème de littérature comparée: les études de thèmes; essai de méthodologie.* Paris: Minard, Lettres Modernes, 1965.

Tseytlin, A.G. "Prestupleniye i nakazaniye i *Les Misérables:* sotsiologicheskiye parallely," *Literatura i marksizm,* No. 5 (1928), pp. 20-58.

Tseytlin, A.G. *Stanovleniye realizma v russkoy literature.* Moscow: Nauka, 1965.

Ubersfeld, Anne. "Le rêve de Jean Valjean," *L'Arc,* 57 (Revue trimestrielle, 1974).

Usakina, Tatyana Ivanovna. *Petrashevtsy i literaturno-obshchestvennoye dvizheniye sorokovykh godov devyatnadtsatogo veka.* Saratov, 1965.

Vidocq. *Mémoires.* Paris: Presses de la Rennaissance, 1970.

Vinogradov, V.V. *Evolyutsiya russkogo naturalizma: Gogol i*

179

Dostoyevski. Leningrad: Akademiya, 1929.

Vogüé, Melchior de. *Le roman russe.* Paris: Plon, Nourrit et Cie, 1886.

Vremya, No. 9 (September, 1862).

Wasiolek, Edward. "On the Structure of *Crime and Punishment,*" *Publications of the Modern Language Association,* Vol. LXXIV (March, 1959), pp. 131-136.

Wasiolek, Edward. *Crime and Punishment and the Critics.* Belmont, California: Wadsworth, 1961.

Wasiolek, Edward. *Dostoevsky: The Major Fiction.* Cambridge, Mass.: M.I.T. Press, 1964.

Weisgerber, Jean. *Faulkner et Dostoievski: Confluences et influences.* Paris: Presses Universitaires de France, 1968.

Wellek, René. "The Crisis in Comparative Literature," *Proceedings of the Second International Congress of Comparative Literature.* Ed. W.P. Friederich. Chapel Hill: University of North Carolina Press, 1959. Reprinted in *Concepts of Criticism,* pp. 282-295.

Wellek, René, ed. *Dostoevsky: A Collection of Critical Essays.* Englewood Cliffs, N.J.: Prentice-Hall, 1962.

Wellek, René. *Concepts of Criticism.* New Haven and London: Yale University Press, 1963.

Wellek, René, and Warren, Austin. *Theory of Literature.* New York: Harcourt, Brace, 1941.

Yakushin, N. *Dostoyevski v Sibiri.* Kemerovo: Kemerovskoye knizhnoye izd-vo, 1960.

Yarmolinsky, Avrahm. *Dostoevsky: His Life and Art.* New York: Criterion Books, 1957.

Zhdanov, Vladimir Viktorovich. *Poety-Petrashevtsy.* Leningrad, 1966.

Zumthor, Paul. *Victor Hugo, poète de Satan.* Paris: Laffont, 1946.

Zumthor, Paul. "Le visionnaire," chap. vi in *Victor Hugo.* ("Collection Génies et Réalités.") Paris: Librairie Hachette, 1967.

Addendum:

Dostoevsky, Fyodor. *The Notebooks for the Brothers Karamazov.* Ed. and tr. Edward Wasiolek. Chicago: University of Chicago Press, 1971.

INDEX

182

183

184

185